LORD
SUGAR

LORD SUGAR

THE MAN WHO REVOLUTIONISED BRITISH BUSINESS

CHARLIE BURDEN

JOHN BLAKE

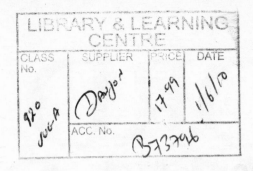
Published by John Blake Publishing Ltd,
3 Bramber Court, 2 Bramber Road,
London W14 9PB, England

www.johnblakepublishing.co.uk

First published in hardback in 2010

ISBN: 978-1-84454-929-0

British Library Cataloguing-in-Publication Data:

A catalogue record for this book is available from the British Library.

Design by www.envydesign.co.uk

Printed in Great Britain by CPI William Clowes Beccles NR34 7TL

1 3 5 7 9 10 8 6 4 2

Papers used by John Blake Publishing are natural, recyclable
products made from wood grown in sustainable forests.
The manufacturing processes conform to the environmental
regulations of the country of origin.

CONTENTS

PROLOGUE

The tranquil, somewhat stuffy surroundings of the Second Chamber had never known anything quite like it.

There was an interested hush as the speaker stood up. 'I'm the new boy on the block in your lordships' house,' he began, adding with a twinkle in his eyes: 'I'm certainly the apprentice.'

Thus did Lord Sugar of Clapton begin his maiden speech to the House of Lords on 25 November 2009. It was a proud and historic event. A memorable one, too. It was as if a lively likely-lad had crashed into a posh old people's home. Sugar was kitted out appropriately, wearing the customary ermine outfit of peers. The man who had risen from an impoverished childhood in the East End of London continued his address by offering the assembled lordships a sense of his family history, served up with another slice of self-deprecating humour thrown in for good measure. It was a story that contrasted greatly with the life experiences of nearly everyone in the chamber.

'I was born into a low-income working class family. We lived in the council estate and I was the youngest of four children. In fact, there was a 12-year gap between me and my elder twin brother and sister. I often joked with my mother that perhaps I was a mistake. She preferred to put it as a pleasant surprise. Some of your lordships may not agree with that.' A few of the peers shifted a little uncomfortably on the chamber's famous red benches.

It had been a similarly mixed reception for Sugar when he first took his seat in the House of Lords five months earlier. On that day he affirmed his allegiance to the Queen, as custom requires, alongside Business Minister Baroness Vadera and Lord Davies of Abersoch. The pair had led him into the Chamber alongside Black Rod, and after the formalities were over Sugar shook hands with Lord Speaker Baroness Hayman. Some of those present claimed they had detected a less welcoming reception for Sugar than is often the case for the arrival of new peers. He then left the Chamber, returned ten minutes later and took his seat on the Labour benches. It would not be until later in the year that he would next speak in the Chamber, on the occasion of his maiden speech, during which he turned effortlessly to the controversy that had greeted his ascent to Government adviser a few months earlier.

That announcement had certainly got the country talking but while many welcomed the move, some found it hard to accept. As ever, the thick-skinned Lord Sugar was the first to acknowledge this. 'On the subject of surprise arrival, I think it is fair to say that my appointment earlier this year as enterprise adviser to this Government was not met with a chorus of wild approval.' It was hard to argue with that, wherever one personally stood on the matter. But it was typical of the man to face this storm head on, rather than hide from it with a tremble. Knowing that one of his most bitter critics in the media was watching from the press gallery, Lord Sugar then dared the doubters to write him off. 'Apart from [the title] Lord Sugar of Clapton I seem to have been awarded another – that of "telly peer",' he said, referring to that critic's words. 'Well, my Lords, with that in mind, those of your lordships who may have stumbled upon the TV show may recall when it started six years ago I made a statement: never, ever underestimate me.' Fighting talk again: this was a confident performance to say the least.

If any of the lordships present were still of a mind to underestimate him, he gave them a neat illustration of his formidable rise to the top. It was one of those passages that polarise opinion: for some it was preening and self promoting, for others it was inspiring and invigorating –

proof that with determination, vision and hard work, anything is possible in Britain. Indeed, the cockney accent with which he delivered the tale of his meritocratic rise to prominence in both business and politics formed an inspiring contrast to the plummy-voiced people around him, with their inherited positions and effortlessly acquired wealth. One hopes his message was not falling on deaf ears. He told them how at the age of 16 he had failed a test as an IBM programmer. 'Twenty or so years later I signed a licence agreement with them because I had captured from them 30 per cent of the European home computer market. And forgive my little boast, my lords, but today I own their European headquarters on the South Bank of the river.'

It was a boast that was derided in some press reports of his speech, but Lord Sugar's words were connecting with the most important audience – the general public. To the people, Sugar's message was full of inspiration. Much of the public has long been sceptical of the Second Chamber's worth. All that inherited power and financial fortune dismays many ordinary working folk of Britain who have to earn every penny. Sugar stands as a motivating champion to those people and, as he told his fellow peers, he earned his fortune not via stock trading or jammy parentage, but by hard work. 'The only hedge fund I ever had was to buy my gardener a new Black and Decker,' he quipped, in a sentiment that sounded not unlike one of his voiceovers during the opening titles of his hit BBC television show *The Apprentice*. Ramming home his point, he said: 'I made [my fortune] by fair and honest and simple trading.'

Then it was time to turn to what he hoped to bring to the country via his new political status. Chief in this would be a renewed round of inspiration and leadership. 'I've spent the past 12 years visiting schools and universities, including the Oxford Union three times and the Cambridge Union twice, and speaking at seminars to the small business community,' he said. During the years of his speeches, he had rarely changed his overall approach. 'My message is: business is hard, it's competitive, but if we are realistic about our weaknesses and strengths we will succeed and create something to be proud of.'

Even those who criticise Sugar would find it hard to dispute that he has, as he said, 'qualities of honesty and straightforwardness'. Indeed, during some of his public appearances in 2009 Sugar was about as forthright in his sentiments as it is possible to imagine, with highly controversial results at times, as we shall see.

During good times and bad Sugar has been a shining beacon of hope to those in Britain who run their own businesses, particularly those whose companies are towards the smaller end of the scale. His backing is sincere and comprehensive: it combines supportive words with tough love. With the recent harsh financial climate, such qualities and contributions are more needed than ever. 'The credit crisis has pushed our SMEs [small- and medium-sized enterprises] to the limit,' he acknowledged. He vowed to help such ventures thrive but impressed on those listening that some of the nation's small businesses would be beyond assistance.

'Some companies struggle not because of failure in their business but because of tougher credit conditions,' he explained. 'The Government has stepped in, as it should, with some temporary schemes.' Then came the harsh sting in the tail, for Lord Sugar is a man who believes many ventures require not a blank cheque but a reality check. 'I have seen some examples of businesses thriving in these difficult times, but I have also seen some poor examples of businesses that simply won't succeed even in the best of times. The reality is, however good the help provided by Government, some businesses don't work. Government and banks can't just write out blank cheques to anyone who thinks they have a good idea.' With a nod to the attention-grabbing headlines that had greeted some of his public speeches, he said: 'I have said this to people who I have met in my recent travels. As I have said, I'm a realist.' Again, few could dispute that.

The speech was nearly over, but Sugar is not one to go quietly. During a rousing conclusion he laid out his vision of himself and his new ennobled role. 'I'm straight, I'm blunt, and I won't always be popular,' he told the Chamber. 'But I promise you this. I will always be honest, and passionate about assisting SMEs and getting our young people to think about business as an opportunity.'

With that, he sat down. However, the ripples from his speech were to continue for days. Sugar has never been a man to stick rigidly to procedures he does not see the value of, but the breaking of a Parliamentary tradition that greeted the end of his maiden speech was a somewhat uncomfortable moment – and it came from one of his opponents.

Lord Oakeshott of the Liberal Democrats was the next to speak, and Lord Sugar got up and left the chamber when he began. The story behind that act had played out over the summer. The pair had exchanged views during recent months after Oakeshott – a privately educated Oxford graduate – was disparaging of Sugar's appointment to the Lords. As Sugar later told a journalist, he felt he came out on top of that particular clash.

'He gave a few TV interviews saying that people like me shouldn't be allowed in the Lords because I supposedly run dodgy businesses and don't pay taxes in the UK – all rubbish, of course,' said Sugar. 'I've spent three months exchanging letters with him until, in the end, he wrote me an apology. Now I feel I've put him in his place.'

However, with the closing words of Sugar's maiden speech still echoing around the halls of Westminster, Oakeshott was about to try and put Sugar in his place. 'I listened to Lord Sugar and his punchy speech after some correspondence with him and his lawyers over the summer. I have apologised to him for any personal distress my comments may have caused and would be happy if he chose to make my whole letter public.' The fiercest words were yet to come.

At this point came the break with convention. Traditionally, peers are not critical of their fellows after their maiden speech, but Oakeshott was not in the mood for tradition and sneered at Sugar and his place in the Lords. 'Lord Sugar is one of our most successful property tycoons with net assets estimated at £730m in this year's *Estates Gazette* rich list,' he said. 'The Amsprop Estates' website displays a fabulous selection of properties from Bond Street to Park Lane, so if he ever gets bored with starring in *The Apprentice* I'm sure he'd be equally brilliant in *Location, Location, Location*.'

The Liberal Democrat peer then described Lord Sugar as 'the most propertied Labour peer in history'. Here, the privileged Oakeshott twisted the knife. 'Isn't it wonderful how well the super-rich, the bankers and the property magnates have done out of the last 12 years of Blair and Brown?' he said, his voice dripping with sarcasm. It had been a pointed and rather sour performance. More in keeping with convention were the words of Lord Wakeham, who said Lord Sugar's speech was 'well received in the House'.

When Lord Sugar returned to the Chamber he was seen speaking – with apparent cordiality – with Lord Oakeshott. But there had never been any illusion that

Sugar would be well received in all corners of the House. Nor would he have cared. For Sugar had not spoken of a craving for the approval of his fellow peers. He was aiming to lay down his mission statement the only way he knew how: in a punchy, attention-grabbing style. If some of the Lords found it uncomfortable (and they did) and if some of the media sneered at his speech in the days to come (and plenty did) then that was fine by him. His appointment had shaken things up in the world of politics. This was fitting because one way or another he has always been a maverick, and a great one at that.

So here it is – the story of how Lord Sugar put the Great back into Britain...

PART ONE

CHAPTER ONE
LORD SUGAR OF CLAPTON

It was an announcement that shook Westminster and much of the nation beyond. Even in the indiscreet and gossipy world of British politics, with its whispering grapevines, anonymous leaks and hushed conversations in dark corridors, there had been little indication of what was to come. The news that broke in June 2008 prompted excited, opinionated discussion: Sir Alan Sugar was to become Lord Sugar.

It was a proud moment for the boy from the East End who could scarcely have dreamed of such a moment during his humble early years in Hackney. The news was all the more surprising because of how well it had been kept under wraps. Only the same day, Sugar himself had been in a television studio giving an interview. Viewers would not have guessed what was about to be revealed later that day. He did not even hint at the sensational news. Only in retrospect was there the slightest indication when he backed Prime Minister Brown who, as usual, was receiving a raft of criticism from opponents and sectors of the media about the state of the economy.

'I am pretty sure that if it was as dire as you are making out he would have done the right thing,' said Sugar. 'He is not going to step down and the reason for that is that he must have the support of the good people and of the right people.' With that he left the studio and waited for the world to learn of his forthcoming political role.

He had been told of the appointment the previous month as he stayed at his plush holiday home in Marbella. A health-conscious man in recent years, he had taken of late to long bike rides, sometimes up to 60 miles. These epic events had given him a lean appearance that contrasted strongly with the more full-faced man who had first come to public attention during the 1980s.

He had set off on his racing bike earlier in the day and as he pumped away at the pedals, his mobile phone rang. It was no ordinary caller: Prime Minister Gordon Brown was waiting on the line for him. The PM explained that he wanted Sugar to join his administration. It was not to be possible to give him a ministerial appointment, because of his widespread business interests. However, the Prime Minister effectively delivered that famous, celebrated message: your country needs you. It was an exciting call-up for the man from Clapton. As Sugar later recalled: 'Gordon said, "I need you to help" and we found a way – with strict guidelines – of making it work.'

Naturally, Sugar had questions about exactly how this would work and there were negotiations to be had, finer details to be agreed. Finally, after some discussion, Sugar accepted the role. It was a wonderful day for the man and his wider family. One of his grandchildren asked him what Lords do. 'So I told him, "We represent the people. We're there to make sure that the Government does what it is supposed to do."'

In handing such a role to Sugar, Brown had appointed a formidable figure. Prior to announcing what name he would take as a peer, there had been discussion as to what his title would be. The *Daily Telegraph*'s City Diary offered humorous odds as to what name he would choose: Lord Sugar of Chigwell at 8/1, Lord Sugar of Epping Forest (Chigwell's parliamentary constituency) 10/1, Lord Sugar of Hackney (his birth place) 16/1, Lord Sugar of Tottenham 18/1 and Lord Amstrad 33/1.

'When the negotiations were done,' he says, 'it brought tears to my eyes. I thought of my mum and dad and growing up in that council house in Clapton… and I decided to call myself Lord Sugar of Clapton.' The man from Hackney, who had been born Alan Sugar and become Sir Alan Sugar, was now going to go one better and become Lord Sugar.

The embattled Prime Minister had turned to Sugar to be his new Enterprise Tsar. What an honour. The news was announced as Gordon Brown reshuffled his cabinet. Sugar was immediately forced to defend his position, denying suggestions that his appointment was merely a publicity stunt. 'It's a shame it looks like that but I'm sure that... you know, I'm not the type of person to be used,' he told the BBC's Andrew Marr. 'I have a passion and commitment to try and help small businesses and enterprise to see if we can get things moving again.'

He later expanded on the reasons for his new direction and his excitement at taking it. 'It has been lacking in the past of people who really know first-hand what is needed in business. I cannot take on a ministerial role and I must not be a person making policy. All I can do is advise those that are in charge of making policy from a business point of view as to what is right and what is wrong. They need someone now in these kind of... emergency economic times that we have got... someone who has been there and worn the T-shirt on what to do as far as business is concerned. That is what interests me most in this thing. I am doing it because of the need of the country really. If you can believe me, it is not politically motivated in any way. It is more I think that small businesses and people need help.'

Who better than Sugar to offer this help? 'With all due respect to the people in Victoria Street, they are what they are – they are civil servants and they have never actually been in business. You have got to have someone there to guide them in the right direction.'

This new position for Sugar cemented the mutual

respect that he and Brown had for one another. In hard times for the economy, the man who had been Chancellor of the Exchequer for just over ten years looked to Sugar as a beacon of hope for the nation's business and finances. In truth, this capped quite a turnabout in the relationship between Sugar and Brown.

Back in March 1992, during the previous recession under Conservative rule, Sugar had written to the *Financial Times* in very disparaging terms. 'I have noted with disgust the comments of a certain Gordon Brown who has accused me of doing well out of the recession,' he wrote angrily. 'I do not know who Mr Gordon Brown is,' he continued. 'Whoever he is, he has not done his homework properly. The man doesn't know what he's talking about. Labour offers no sort of route out of recession.'

Hardly the words one would expect to herald a bright new relationship. However, five years later, with Labour now in power, the pair met in the flesh at a football match between Coventry City and Tottenham Hotspur. Any awkwardness over Sugar's earlier remarks was quickly dispelled by the rapport they struck up and the ideas they discussed. It proved a meeting of minds, and more important matters than the beautiful game were on the agenda.

'I said to him I'd be interested in embarking on visits to schools and from that moment onwards I've been to every single university in the land.' Now, 12 years on from that football match chat, here he was, invited into the corridors of power by none other than Gordon Brown to help him steer the country out of recession. Presumably now Sugar felt that Brown had 'done his homework properly'. In accepting the invitation, Sugar reprised his 'I don't know him' line but directed it this time at Conservative leader David Cameron. Asked by the BBC if he would retain his position under a possible future Conservative Government under Mr Cameron, Sugar replied, 'I have never met Mr Cameron and I don't know anything about him.'

In truth, Sugar had been backing Brown soon after he entered 10 Downing Street as Prime Minister. It had been a tough start to Brown's reign, with the country facing numerous trials in the opening weeks and months of his administration, including flooding, a fresh outbreak of foot-and-mouth disease and terror attacks in London and Scotland. As these horrors were taking place, there was a backdrop of rumours that members of Brown's own cabinet were plotting against the new leader.

Sugar was appalled by this treachery. 'You can't run a Government and you can't run a company or anything like that unless everybody is on side,' he said. 'If they are not on side [Brown] should kick them out, and then what he should do is tell the rest of the world that he has been appointed to do a job for two years and let me get on with it and then at the end of that period of time – judge me then. It's very easy for people to blame the top man when things are no good but you have to look deeper at what these problems are.' He was proving a fine ally to the under-fire Brown, who could scarcely have imagined the problems he would face as Prime Minister during those long years of waiting for Tony Blair to hand over the reins of power.

In backing the new Prime Minister Sugar was at pains to stress that his support was not a new affair, despite their differences all those years ago. 'It's not just recently that I have backed Gordon Brown,' he insisted. 'I've known him for a long time as Chancellor and I have got to know him quite well. Out of the last four prime ministers that I have had the pleasure to have met I think he is a very, very clever man and a man who is over everything and knows what is going on.'

Many have attacked Brown as lacking charisma by comparison with his predecessor Tony Blair and the opposition leader David Cameron. For Sugar this was a positive thing. 'He may not come across as some kind of actor but he has got his hand on the pulse,' he roared. This stance is entirely fitting: Sugar has rarely worried about the niceties of spin and chasing public approval. It is no wonder that he would be more impressed by the down-to-earth Brown than the showbusiness style of Blair.

Sugar insisted that he had no need to be positive about Brown and that he would never be blindly positive or grovel to any politician. His conviction in this regard could scarcely be stronger. 'I have no axe to grind. Let's face it, I have done OK – I am Sir Alan, recognised by the Queen for my services to business thanks to my natural-born entrepreneurial spirit. You haven't seen me up the arse of the politicians. I don't need to achieve anything or be recognised any more.' It is certainly hard to imagine the scowling figure from *The Apprentice* smooth-talking his way into politics. Indeed, he did not envy Brown his job. Watching the flack that the new PM was attracting, Sugar could not help but remember the times when he'd faced criticism. It could be lonely at the top in his own fields.

'It reminds me of my days as a football club chairman,' said Sir Alan of Brown's experiences. (Sugar was chairman of Tottenham Hotspur from 1991 to 2001.) 'Walk out of the ground after giving the opponents a good hiding and the fans would shout: "Alwight, Al" ... "top man" ... "keep up the good work, mate" ... "how's the family?" ... "well done, son"... A week later when we got our arse kicked the same group shouted: "Oi, you tosser, what you gonna do about the team then, eh?" ... "get your f***ing chequebook out, you f***ing w******"...' Indeed, many have remarked that there are similarities between the role of the football manager and that of Prime Minister. Both jobs carry weighty responsibility in the eyes of the people of the nation who all too often believe they could do better than the incumbent.

If there was a dose of irony to his and Brown's newfound mutual respect, it was lost on those who decided to question the appointment in more direct terms. Sugar has always been one whose mere existence seems to ruffle the feathers of some. He has often divided opinions on both sides. His entry into politics was to prove no different and soon after the announcement he was given a crash-course in the harshness of Westminster life when Baroness Prosser, who had been Labour Party treasurer in the second half of the 1990s, publicly condemned his appointment.

'I am completely astonished that we would think that Alan Sugar is a suitable person to be a spokesman for the British Government,' she declared. 'He is a person who promotes via his television programme a style of management that is about bullying and sexism. If anyone thinks that's appropriate or if anybody even thinks that's how management works in reality then they are in a world far different from mine. I just think it is a very bad thing to have done. We're talking about somebody whose style is completely at odds with the ethics of what I consider to be the true Labour movement.'

She was not the only Labour peer to have issues with Sugar being awarded that role. Lord Evans of Temple Guiting said: 'He does not represent in any way anything I think about the Labour Government. For a man to be given a peerage whose public image is that of a TV bully saying "You're fired" – well, I don't understand how it happened. Whose decision was it? Who said, "What a jolly good idea, make him a peer"?'

That such attacks were coming from the Labour side of the fence made them particularly regrettable. Naturally,

Conservative leader David Cameron took a swipe at Brown's administration, too. Referring to the changes in the Cabinet that brought Sugar in, he said of the Prime Minister: 'He is not reshuffling the Cabinet, the Cabinet is reshuffling him. If he cannot run the Cabinet, how can he run the country? All roads now should lead towards a General Election.' The *Daily Mail*'s columnist Peter McKay joined in the criticism, writing of Brown's moves and turning his infamous scorn against Lord Sugar by implication: 'He thinks that associating himself with TV shows and performers endears him to voters.'

The criticism came from more considered newspaper writers too. Rachel Sylvester of the *Daily Telegraph* was dismissive. 'Civil servants and business people just find the appointment embarrassing,' wrote the political scribe. 'The Prime Minister sees himself as Mary Poppins, giving voters a spoonful of Sugar to help the recession medicine go down – but in fact he is like a man handing out Yorkie bars which bear the slogan "not for girls".'

Sylvester also delved into the past for support for her views, as she recalled an interview with Sugar in 2008, in which she felt he had not shown the right views and attitudes to become a part of Brown's Government. 'He [Sugar] also insisted that "there's nothing wrong with being greedy", that human rights are "rubbish" and that "this Government's not Labour, it's old-fashioned Tory",' she wrote. 'Are these really opinions that Mr Brown wants to reward with a seat in Parliament? I would love to hear the Prime Minister's Enterprise Tsar debating work-life balance with Harriet Harman.'

In time plenty more would have their say, both on the printed page and on the benches of Parliament. It was to prove a testing time for Lord Sugar. *The Times* newspaper gave over its leader page editorial on 21 July 2009 to Sugar's appointment. 'However, Gordon Brown has not just appointed ... Lord Sugar to his administration. He has also appointed him directly to the legislature. He has done this with hardly any scrutiny, with no voting and with no debate.' Pressing the case for confirmation hearings to take place before peerages were finalised, it continued, 'Nothing calls more loudly for the institution of confirmation hearings than Lord Sugar's appointment. Until such a change is made, the process for appointing outsiders to Government will remain as idiosyncratic and undemocratic as Lord Sugar's selection of his apprentice. And it is commonly remarked that he often gets these choices wrong.'

Harsh words and a far cry from the welcome that Sugar might have hoped for, though he is no fool and will surely have expected a barrage of fire. He kept his dignity in the face of growing attacks but Sugar has always been a tough man and more than equipped to defend himself. Explaining his appointment, he said the Government had 'been lacking people who know first-hand what is needed in business'.

Baroness Prosser's words were drowned out by others in the Labour movement. Business Secretary Lord

Mandelson was one of those who expressed a support for the appointment. He said: 'Lord Sugar is just one heck of a man and you will see him pioneering enterprise, backing small and medium-sized enterprises around the country. That's what we need. If we are going to succeed economically in this country, we are going to have that sort of success and Alan Sugar's going to help us achieve it.'

Indeed, Sugar found it easy to brush off the criticisms of others, particularly from Tory leader David Cameron, a man he had form with when it came to public clashes. Sugar had won the bout each time.

In September 2008, Cameron told a journalist that he was not a fan of Sir Alan, nor his television show. 'I hate both of them,' he growled. 'I can't bear Alan Sugar. I like TV to escape.' Sir Alan was masterfully cutting in his response. 'I'm glad he can't bear me,' he said. 'Perhaps he will stop asking people to sound me out if I want to meet him and defect to his party.' Piling on the embarrassment for Cameron, he also accused the opposition leader of hiding from difficult questions during the harsh financial climate. 'I am still waiting for him to answer my question: If he was in power, would things be any different?' asked Sugar. 'He seems to know when to stay silent.'

At the same time a BBC poll was suggesting that the public trusted Brown more than Cameron, so Sugar's words reflected a public frustration with the Tory leader. The newspapers loved Sugar's smart response, with one tabloid headlining its story SIR ALAN EXPOSES TORY

LEADER CAM AS A SHAM. The broadsheets, too, enjoyed it, with *The Times* concluding: 'With dust-ups like this, who needs reality TV?' If the war of words between Sugar and Cameron had been an *Apprentice* task, it would have been the Tory leader taking the walk of shame to the taxi at the end of it. Certainly, Cameron must have wished he had never opened his mouth and his words were notably more measured when he questioned Sugar's appointment in 2009.

There were other humorous words on Sugar's elevation. The *Sunday Times* imagined Sugar at Downing Street, announcing the details of a new *Apprentice*-style task with Gordon Brown as the main contestant. 'Your task today is to design a new cabinet from scratch,' the newspaper had him saying. 'The winners will be the team that completes the task while paying the smallest political price. A word of warning, though: in this task, there is no winner.' When the new cabinet is completed and presented to Sugar, the paper joked, he would be distinctly unimpressed.

He asks Brown: 'What's that supposed to be?' and Brown tells him it is a new 'radical' cabinet. 'But it looks exactly like the old one, only worse. It's pathetic. I gave you a chance, Gordon, and you've blown it. You can't build a cabinet, your advertising on YouTube was a complete bloody joke and you've upset all the women in your team. I don't want to hear any more excuses. Gordon – you're fired.'

As we shall see throughout these pages, Lord Sugar's *Apprentice* catchphrase is in danger of being worn out by those who write about him as they grope for a handy sign-off to their gags. Indeed, the man himself has pushed to have the chance to vary the phrasing he uses as he dismisses *Apprentice* candidates. 'Personally, I'd have liked the flexibility to be able to vary it, to say "you're sacked" or "get out" or possibly even "clear off",' he shrugs. 'But they tell me "you're fired" is great TV.' It is now a phrase he will never be able to shrug off.

Increased hostility from the press was something Lord Sugar would have to become accustomed to in politics. Not that this was anything new. He remembers how, at the age of 15, he became properly aware of the political scene and the office of Prime Minister in particular. 'It was the first time I signed on to why the country needs a leader,' he explained. This, however, did not signify automatic respect from Sugar for the men who filled the role. Echoing his respect for leaders who eschew showbiz popularity in favour of good, sensible politics, he added: 'In those days a Prime Minister was seen as stuffy, perhaps boring, but a serious person – a person you trusted to guide the country through the challenges it faced both at home and abroad.' For many of the public Sugar's preference for a reliable, old-fashioned politician ahead of a showbiz version will ring true. After spin dominated the 1990s and beyond, people want what Sugar wants and offers: sincerity ahead of celebrity.

Sugar's first involvement in the ways of Westminster came several decades ago. He first walked the corridors of Whitehall in the 1960s, when he took a job in the civil service as a statistician at the Ministry of Education and Science. If this seems an unlikely path – full of red-tape, onerous procedures and jobsworths – for a man like Sugar to take, then that's because it is. 'It bores me talking about it again and again,' he says now. He took it simply as a result of what he had and had not enjoyed during his schooling. 'Science – this was something I had always been interested it. Statistics, maths – I wasn't too bad at that. So I thought I'd go for it.' He found the deskbound job to be 'total agony', however, and could not wait for each working day to end so he could get home. So dull was the work, he recalls, that the task of calculating what percentage of schoolchildren drank milk in the morning was one of the more exciting tasks. 'Imagine my disappointment when I was plonked into a boring office, pushing a load of paper around,' he remembered. He sat each day, waiting for the clock to hit 5pm.

After a year he decided to leave for good. His mother summed up the problem succinctly: her son did not like it, she said, because it was 'a sitting-down job'. It had not been a successful introduction to the ways of politics.

Not that it was enough to put him off Westminster. Since the 1980s, he has flirted with the world of politics. This has always been essentially a two-way flirtation but it was often the case that it was the world of politics making overtures to Sugar, rather than vice versa. Sugar was more the chased than the chaser.

First, he worked for Business In The Community (BITC). Formed in 1982, BITC was launched in the wake of the Toxteth and Brixton riots which had shone such a distressing light upon the social problems blighting the lives of people in the UK's more deprived communities. In the previous decade in America, business leaders had helped to regenerate areas such as Baltimore and Detroit. It had worked well and it was this example that BITC wanted to follow in Britain. Those quick to back the initiative included Barclays Bank, BP, British Steel, IBM, ICI, Marks & Spencer, Midland Bank and WHSmith. By 1985 there were over 108 member companies and HRH The Prince of Wales got on board as the organisation's president.

It was alongside the Prince of Wales that one of Sugar's first involvements took place. They travelled to Hartlepool in the north-east of England, an area with terribly high unemployment levels. There they met hordes of jobless locals, many of them young men. Sugar was transported back to his East End childhood, and through this prism saw the situation in family terms. His job was to encourage these disillusioned, desperate locals to follow his example and not the example set by his own father, who was never assured enough to launch his own business.

Looking back later, he recalled his conversations with the people of Hartlepool. '[I told them] they could become gardeners, window cleaners, painters and decorators,' he said. 'Perhaps some of them might even be able to employ one or two other people. I suggested they should have the confidence to think of starting up their own business.'

It was an inspiring message and an authentic one coming from Sugar. A man who had no silver spoon in his mouth and no inherent privilege (unlike his royal travelling companion) was showing similar people what could be done with a bit of hard work and confidence. He has since returned to the north-east to repeat the same message. In September 2009 he lent his weight to a new market being launched in Hartlepool. 'Initiatives like this all help in increasing interest in business and encourage entrepreneurs and future entrepreneurs to achieve their goals. We need entrepreneurs now more than ever to make sure businesses survive these difficult times and are able to fully exploit the opportunities of tomorrow. I wish the organisers and stallholders in Hartlepool every success.' With his best wishes they have a good chance.

However, back in the 1980s he was still building his own confidence to make such appearances. Slowly, his levels of self-belief rose and he felt more inclined to take on new challenges. As the decade neared its end, he was ready to broaden the scope of his public and political work. In 1988 he was invited to take on a starring role in a new Government advertising initiative. The campaign was to promote public awareness of increasing integration in the European business world. Trade barriers were coming down across the continent and the Government wanted to rejuvenate business by reminding the businessmen and women of the nation of this fact. The Trade and Industry Secretary, Lord Young, was determined to get the great and the good of British business to assist with the campaign. He approached Virgin supremo Richard Branson, ICI boss Sir John-Harvey Jones, Jaguar saviour Sir John Egan and others. Those others included Sugar, a man who Lord Young had long been a fan of.

'He's one of a new breed of British entrepreneurs,' said Young of Sugar. 'I would like to see people as role models for young people coming into business. I want people to say "Damn it, if he can do it, I can."' Speaking of the group of businessmen he had assembled for the advertising campaign, Young had particular praise for Sugar. 'All of them were people who stood out above the crowd,' he beamed. 'There's no question that Alan Sugar was the foremost British leader in the computer industry and electronics goods generally.' It was this respect from Lord Young that earned Sugar the invitation. However, once he was signed up it was clear that Sugar was going to be somewhat leftfield in his approach to the project. When handed the script for his part of the television slot he was rather unimpressed by what he read. He felt it was stale and inappropriate for him.

Keen to take part in a commercial that played to his strengths, Sugar rang Young direct and told him that he wanted to re-write the script himself. Showing the sort of grasp of the television medium that would make him such a star on *The Apprentice*, Sugar sat down and put together a more punchy script for the commercial and one that pleased Young. Not that the Secretary had ever had serious doubts about Sugar's ability to deliver. 'I thought that since he knew a thing or two about marketing I wouldn't worry,' he said of his decision to allow Sugar to rework the script. His hunch was rewarded when Sugar sent him a script that showed a definite knack for television work. In Sugar's version, the supremo would stand next to a set of Amstrad computers marked for despatch to different parts of Europe and explain to the camera that, under new trading rules, he would no longer have to adapt the computers for each of the different countries' markets. He then explained what this meant for a business such as his.

This was the version that was filmed and put out by the Government. After the set of advertisements had been broadcast, research was carried out to see which of them had worked best. Sugar's one stood proudly near the top of that chart. He had connected with the business public in a way rarely matched by the others who Young had hired to take part in the consciousness-raising exercise. Here was a sign as early as 1988 that he would have a great future in the worlds of both politics and television. The political hue of the Government might change and television was to alter dramatically over the coming decades, but Sugar would keep his place in both spheres. Indeed, he would become a key member of both worlds, famous and revered throughout his land.

In the wake of this triumph and of his BITC engagement alongside the Prince of Wales, Sugar was invited to more and more prestigious affairs, including events at 10 Downing Street and Buckingham Palace. The Hackney boy had grown into a man who was not out of place at the two most powerful, prestigious addresses in the UK. How proud he must have been as he realised that Britain's leaders wanted to invite him to their residences. It would be 20 years before he was officially welcomed into the very highest corridors of power as Gordon Brown's Enterprise Tsar. However, he was on his way to the top. At one of the Downing Street events he got talking with Lord Young, who noticed a trend in the way that Sugar's working life was developing. Young observed the way the political and business sides of his colleague's career were standing and demonstrated an accurate eye for assessing Sugar's present and the future.

'I suppose during the early years of the decade, up to 1986 or 1987, Sugar was riding a tiger which was almost impossible to control,' he told author David Thomas. 'Then, just when it's established and he's worth several hundred million pounds, Amstrad develops some problems. He's got to overcome those. But by the early 1990s, the problems could be behind him and he's got a steady business which is growing fast. It may come to the stage when it's not a 24-hour-a-day job to run his business. Then he may look for other things to do. It may be charitable or political activities.'

Sugar was of course to become involved in both such activities. His charitable work is outlined in full in another chapter. Young felt that for the moment, Sugar's roots made him feel at times uncomfortable as he began to dip his toe into the weird world of Westminster. 'He's still, I think, got a slight air of insecurity about him,' observed Young. 'He hasn't shown any sign of wanting to come into the fold. That may happen later on, perhaps when he's Sir Alan Sugar, or Lord Sugar of Chigwell, or whatever else happens in their dotage to great industrialists. Who can tell? He may not. He's never struck me as the sort of person who sets great store on being a member of the establishment.'

What accurate and prescient words these were. Sugar has never been entirely comfortable with his place in politics, and has never desperately scrambled for a place at its top table as others have. It is this dichotomy in his relationship with political power that makes him such a suitable candidate to work within that sphere. A business supremo who showed more eagerness or even desperation to get into politics would surely be too keen and as such subject to understandable suspicion. Just as the Speaker of the House of Commons by tradition accepts the role reluctantly – when the Speaker first takes up the role, he or she is by custom literally dragged to the Speaker's chair by colleagues – Sugar has never been one to court a political role. As Young's words from the 1980s show, he was essentially reluctant and suspicious back then too.

Ironically, given his place at the power table of a Labour administration, Lord Sugar was a Conservative voter in the 1980s. 'I voted for Thatcher,' he confirmed. 'I admired her, letting cheeky chappies like me come into a marketplace which was normally riddled with the elite. My worry about the [Conservative] opposition party now is that we're going back to those days.'

Asked whether he would consider working with a future Conservative Government, he confirmed he would if the role offered was suitable. 'If anybody approached me to say would I continue supporting small- and medium-sized businesses, I would say "yes". I would continue my role under any Government,' he said. As to whether he thought such an approach was likely, Sugar was less than convinced. He said there was as much chance of that as 'a rabbi eating a bacon sandwich. They wouldn't out of sheer belligerence, even if I was the best bloke in the country.'

The Conservatives were soon causing trouble in the wake of Sugar's appointment, suggesting that he could no longer be the star of the BBC reality show *The Apprentice*, as his political role ruled him out of being impartial. An investigation was launched. A BBC spokesman concluded:

'Following detailed discussions with Sir Alan Sugar, the BBC is satisfied that his new role as an enterprise champion to the Government will not compromise the BBC's impartiality or his ability to present *The Apprentice*. Sir Alan is not going to be making policy for the Government, nor does he have a duty to endorse Government policy. Moreover, Sir Alan has agreed that he will suspend all public-facing activity relating to this unpaid post in the lead up to and during any shows that he is presenting on the BBC. Should he be offered a peerage Sir Alan will also be free to join other peers who do work for the BBC including Lord Lloyd Webber, Lord Bragg and Lord Winston in the House of Lords.'

However, in November 2009 there was one change to *The Apprentice* made in response to Lord Sugar's political appointment. The BBC announced that rather than run the new series in the spring as normal, they would postpone it until the summer. The sixth series was due to kick-off in March 2010 but the BBC moved it to 3 June so it would be broadcast after the latest date on which the General Election could be held. This came after the BBC Trust ruled there would be an 'increased risk to impartiality'. Lord Sugar was not happy with the decision, which he felt came after undue pressure on the BBC from the Conservative Party.

'They've delayed it for some political reason, which is a bit of a joke in my opinion,' he said. 'Somebody from the Tory party complained to the BBC about me being an adviser to the Government and the result is that the television programme can't be transmitted until the General Election is over.' He was dismayed by this and pointed his famous forefinger firmly in the direction of the Conservatives in suggesting who was to blame. 'It is very frustrating because the programme itself has got nothing in it that is political at all, but unfortunately the BBC are frightened of the Tory party. They've been bullied by the Tory party and they can't stand up to common sense.'

There were inevitable changes, though, to Sugar's life as this new political chapter dawned in his story. He was dropped as the face of the Government's multi-million pound National Savings and Investments advertising campaign. 'This is as per Cabinet Office rules, which prohibit the use of political figures in Government advertising,' explained a spokesman for NS&I. Sugar added that there was no issue regarding his fee for the campaign, because he had in any case donated it to his charitable trust, of which the Great Ormond Street Hospital for Children is a major beneficiary. As we shall see in the charity chapter, Sugar's generosity is enormous, benefiting numerous good causes.

Sugar's popularity is also enormous, crossing generations. In 2009, British schoolchildren aged between nine and 11 were polled about who would make an ideal head teacher. Some of the results were predictable: *Doctor Who* star David Tennant came top of the poll, ahead of the likes of JK Rowling, Cheryl Cole and David Beckham. However, at number eight – ahead of Formula 1 driver Lewis Hamilton – came Lord Sugar. Indeed, in 2008 he had finished at the top of a poll of the British public to create a dream cabinet. Some three thousand people were asked to name who they thought would be ideal for each of the cabinet roles, from Home Secretary to Chancellor and Prime Minister. In the poll results, Terry Wogan was named Home Secretary, Gordon Ramsay made Minister for Health and Jeremy Clarkson was put in charge of transport. Stephen Fry was favourite for Deputy PM, former *Countdown* numbers genius Carol Vorderman was Chancellor of the Exchequer and Bono of U2 and Michael Palin would jointly run the Foreign Office. The role of Prime Minister was awarded to Sir Alan Sugar.

In real life, it was being widely suggested that Sugar's peerage was given to him as a result of his celebrity. To students of politics, this was nothing new: Sugar was merely the latest person to become one of what the media have been calling GOATS – the acronym for the 'Government Of All Talents'. This was not an entirely modern development. In 1914, for instance, Lord Kitchener was made war minister and later in the century media magnate Lord Beaverbrook and union boss Ernest Bevin also crossed into Westminster. More recently, Brown's predecessor Tony Blair had given peerages to Lords Sainsbury, Simon and Adonis. Now surgeon Lord

Darzi, ex CBI-director Digby Jones and Admiral Alan West all took roles in Brown's regime. Opinion was divided in the corridors of power as to whether this tactic was a good thing. Certainly, not all hung around long, turning from 'goats' into 'escape goats'. When some of the above departed swiftly, some in politics felt vindicated. 'It's not as easy as it looks, is it?' they sniffed. Inevitably, some predicted that Sugar would not be a GOAT for long either.

However, Sugar's passion and vision for politics is no flash in the-pan affair. For so long he has watched the direction that Britain is heading in and felt disapproval. Along with this, he has always held strong opinions on how to fix the nation's problems. He has been particularly outspoken on crime, especially the striking rise in violent crime among the youth of today. 'It's beyond my comprehension that I hear every day of someone being stabbed,' he says. 'It's like the weather. You know it's going to happen, you just read to find out the details. It has gone bloody mad out there. It really is broken Britain. Something needs to be done and it has got to be radical. No half measures. If it were up to me I'd use a sledgehammer to crack a nut. The Government needs to invest more money in the police force. And I'm not talking about a couple of extra bobbies on the beat in each borough. I'm talking about real investment.'

Sugar entered a political world that was losing more and more of the public's trust with each passing year. In

2008 and 2009 the scandal of expenses erupted in Westminster. With the media fanning the flames, the politicians of Britain woke up each day to the increasing anger of the public after some were exposed to have bent the rules about allowances. By the time the main body of the scandal was over, several MPs had been sacked or had resigned. The public fury turned quickly into renewed cynicism about their Members of Parliament. Sugar entered politics as the aftershock of the dark affair was still resonating. He was clear about how he would avoid getting caught up in similar trouble himself.

'I've told them that I will not be taking a penny in expenses,' he said. 'Do you think I want to get involved in all that? Peers are entitled to a certain amount of money for every day they turn up here as well as a refund on parking, but even if I had a genuine expense I would never claim it: it's not worth the aggravation. More importantly, I don't need the money.'

Indeed he doesn't, with a personal fortune estimated to be in excess of £800 million. It is not just that he does not need to bend any rules: he can also bring specialist insight to the table as a result of what he learned acquiring all that wealth. 'I've made my money,' he said. 'I've employed thousands in my time and what I'm passionate about now is helping out the small businesses which make up over 50 per cent of the economy of this country. There isn't anyone in the Government who knows as much about this as I do. When I first got involved in the football industry, it was similar to my arrival here – the elite group of chairmen made me feel like Vivian Malone Jones, the first black student to enter the University of Alabama in 1963, but I made my mark.'

His allusion to racial prejudice is a highly valid and revealing one. There is undoubtedly a strain of anti-Semitism in some of the dislike felt for Lord Sugar in some quarters in England. 'The Jew [in England] is portrayed as Fagin, and you won't shake that out of people's heads,' he once told the Israeli newspaper *Ha'aretz*. 'It's an underlying thing – that the Jews are a little bit sharp, a little bit quick, not to be trusted, possibly. If you ask a group of non-Jews in a pub what it is that they don't like about Jews, this is what they'll come out with... that they hoard money.' If financial envy is at the heart of some anti-Jewish prejudice, then that envy must be felt all the more keenly towards Lord Sugar thanks to his huge financial success.

There is also, perhaps, a slice of snobbery too. For the working people of Britain Lord Sugar is, in most cases, the hero from Hackney, but for others his background is a source of distaste. It's something he is used to: in the 1970s a trade journalist explained that Sugar's business was 'quite frankly rather looked down upon by the serious side of the industry... he had all the appearance and trappings of the back-street marketer.' However, says the same commentator, within a few years perceptions of Sugar had turned around. 'Suddenly we were aware of the fact that this back-street trader was one of the most significant people in the industry.'

Some people still believe that men from his neck of woods have no place in the upper echelons of business, much less the House of Lords. Is Sugar bothered? He could hardly be less so. Rightly proud of his background, Sugar feels it has positively shaped the way he is as a man. 'I can't help the way I am,' he states firmly. Indeed, he wonders, why would he want to? 'My East End background might have made me a little rough round the edges, but that's not something I can do anything about. It was good training for reality; it kept me down-to-earth and taught me to quickly appraise situations and assess propositions.'

No wonder people flock to listen to his talks about business – his is an inspiring tale. 'I fought my way out of poverty and I remain convinced that others can do likewise, too,' he said. Not that he is disparaging of the environment in which he grew up. Indeed, he looks back at it rather romantically. 'We lived in the council blocks and we did all the good things,' he said. 'You could play in the streets, playgrounds, build bikes and carts. You can't roam around in these terrible times we live in now.'

During the 1980s an Australian journalist observed Sugar at close quarters and concluded that snobbery was definitely at work in some people's perceptions of him. Gareth Powell, of the *Sydney Morning Herald*, wrote: 'Sugar has spice, but he is not quite nice. At least this is the attitude of the computer journalists in Britain.' After closer examination, Powell concluded that much of the criticism of him was unfair. 'In the past few weeks,' he wrote, 'I have been told by journalists that Sugar is a "business thug", whatever that may mean, and that he is never seen in public without two bodyguards.' However, when Powell encountered Sugar at a public press conference, he said no bodyguards were to be seen and that numerous enquiries failed to produce any proof that Sugar employed bodyguards at all. Powell concluded that jealousy and snobbery were largely to blame, together with a very English suspicion of success.

Not that Sugar is romantic about his background in a naive way. Indeed, he is damning of people from Hackney who approach him believing that they automatically have a connection merely because they come from – or at least claim to come from – the same borough. 'You can see them coming from the corner of your eye. He or she has been staring at you all night. No, not plucking up courage – these people are the worst, they are rude, they butt in, they have no common courtesy at all. They say something like, "You know my uncle in Hackney." I say, "Oh, really?" "Yes, he says you know him very well." Then they rattle off a name. I say, "No, I don't know him. I've never heard of him." "Oh, but you do know him." "I don't know him, I'm sorry." "But you went to school with him, you must know him." Then I get a bit annoyed. Yes, sometimes I can be rude. I would probably say, "Well, I don't know him, so clear off" – or words to that effect.'

As he said in his maiden speech, the Lords and the public at large underestimate him at their peril. In a time of economic uncertainty and a recession which has terrified and hurt many Britons, Lord Sugar has exactly the kind of spirit which can get not just the economy going once more but also the confidence of the nation. He represents many of the key values that made Britain what it once was, and what so many wish it to become again.

Next we'll examine each of those traits and show how Lord Sugar has them in spades, making him the man to put the Great back into Britain. From enterprise to charity, leadership to family values, via entertainment, honesty and so much more – Lord Sugar's story will be examined via the greatest of qualities.

We'll also assess where Lord Sugar stands in 2010 and look to his future. How will his life develop politically, in business and personally? First, though, let's examine those qualities that he has in such abundance.

PART TWO

CHAPTER ONE
HONESTY

The fact that Lord Sugar has been in business for four decades and not even the most ferocious and cynical of journalists have been able to pin any suggestion of wrong-doing onto him speaks volumes for his honesty. After all, business is a bruising, fierce and competitive arena, as Sugar discovered from the off. 'I was competing against 40 other small-time dealers [in the hi-fi market], who'd kill their grandmothers in order to beat me to a deal,' he said of his early days.

Then came diversification as Amstrad stepped into more markets. He has also endured torrid years in football, a sphere he found riddled with dishonesty. Yet for all the cynics who regularly hurl abuse at Sugar and for all the controversy surrounding his views in certain areas, nobody has ever been able to present him as anything less than an honest businessman.

That said, the word honest can sometimes be another way of saying harsh. This is something that the Labour administration was only too aware of in 2009. 'People respect the advice he gives them, even if it's harsh sometimes,' said Gordon Brown when he ennobled Lord Sugar. How right he was, as was proved in the subsequent months. Sugar would be harsh at times as he appeared at a series of public events across the UK. If Mr Brown's administration were under any illusions about the extent of their new man's straight, honest talking then they were given a wake-up call in November 2009 when he and Business Secretary Lord Mandelson attended an event in Manchester.

It was a question and answer session for bosses of small- to medium-sized businesses. Sugar is very much the man for such an event, having once stood in the shoes of those bosses before rising to a level of success and riches that they could only dream of. It is true that he was on their side, not least during these testing financial times, but that was never going to mean that he would quietly and politely smooth over any difficult issues that might be raised during the session. He would not patronise them by giving them anything less than the honest truth as businessman Alber Goldberg discovered when he spoke from the floor.

Goldberg, who runs a Blackpool-based company that provides luminous paint for glow-in-the-dark ceilings, complained that four separate banks had refused to give him a loan to develop new products in his business. Lord Sugar replied: 'I hate the use of this word cash-flow in the sense that it is a business problem. Banks are there to do business. Anyone who says they are not is wrong. I can honestly say a lot of problems you hear from people who are moaning are from companies I wouldn't lend a penny to. They are bust. The moaners are bust. They are bust and they don't need the bank – they need an insolvency practitioner.' That was certainly straight to the point, but Sugar was about to get even closer to the bone. 'I would look at you right in the eyes and tell you out of 100 complaints, on investigation I would say 15 of them had something to moan about,' he told the audience, many of whom shuffled very uncomfortably in their seats.

In a familiar echo of the speech he gave to City University in the 1980s, Lord Sugar then turned his attention to the younger members of the audience. These were the business people who had not lived through a previous recession and had no experience of working under a testing financial situation. He warned them not to expect to just be handed credit on a plate, as they might have been prior to the banks tightening their belts. 'The problem is that some younger people who have lived through the last ten years or so of business – and prior to that ten years they may have just come from education – they think the irresponsible manner in which the banks dealt is the norm. Let me tell you, you lived in the Disneyworld, you have lived in the unrealistic

Disneyworld in the way banks dished out money.' It was a phrase that would come back to haunt him, but he could not know that then.

'I have been in this position of advising the Government since June of this year,' he continued, 'and I have listened to a lot of the business link centres. In doing so I have insisted on meeting the business advisers and listened to the advice they are giving. On top of the list of complaints were banks: "The bank won't do this, the bank won't do that."'

If some of the 400-strong audience at the Hilton Manchester Deansgate Hotel were feeling uncomfortable, Sugar's co-speaker Mandelson was about to feel the heat, too. 'There's a situation caused by the Government themselves in a message they put out last year after they lent the £3 trillion [sic] to the banks. "We'll lend you the money but you have got to lend it out to businesses."' The effect, Sugar argued, was false expectations. 'I think that got misunderstood by a lot of people who thought they could just walk up to the wall somewhere, press some numbers in and cash was going to come out of the wall,' he added.

The event caused a stir, just as his famous City University appearance had three decades earlier. Alber Goldberg was certainly shaken and stirred by Sugar's response to his question. 'I love watching him on *The Apprentice*, but that was out of order – I was just asking a question, then *boom*!' he complained. Some national newspapers reported the event, and Sugar's words, as if it had been a hostile, unsuccessful occasion.

At a similar event in the East Midlands the previous week an audience member had complained about a response Sugar had given to her question. She asked how she could expand her cake-making business without coming off the state benefits that she had begun to take after her husband had lost his job months previously. The rules of the benefit system limited the amount of hours that she was allowed to work each week. Sugar suggested she come off benefits and work full-time on making the business prosper. She replied that she could not afford to take this step. 'If you wish to remain on the benefit system that's your decision,' said Sugar. 'What am I supposed to do, wave a wand and change the benefits system? You could buy three ovens, food mixers and then in 24 hours you could make more cakes. But you will say you don't have enough money for that. What am I supposed to do? It's the magic wand again,' he said.

The unnamed woman was unhappy with Sugar's response and complained to the press afterwards. She said: 'I felt he was inappropriate for somebody who was there in his role as government adviser. I thought he would have had something practical to say like, concentrate on producing the goods or put an hour aside to make sure your books are up to date. I was completely taken aback.'

This suggested a rather thin skin on her part, because

the entire premise of her question was that she was in an impossible situation given the current rules of the benefit system. To expect Sugar's response to not reflect the same truth was perhaps over-optimistic. A spokesman for Lord Sugar said: 'The woman presented Lord Sugar with an unsolvable problem and was aware of this when she put the question. Lord Sugar explained that if she was unable to give up the benefits, then her problem was impossible to solve unless, for example, she bought additional cooking and mixing machines so that in the hours she was allowed to work she could make more cakes. She answered that she works from her small kitchen at home. The woman took exception to the answer and interpreted it that Lord Sugar said she should remain on benefits. It was clear to the whole audience what Lord Sugar said, and many people were surprised at her attitude. She presented a situation designed to be unsolvable unless she was prepared to take the risk of expanding and, if she was confident in herself and business, then that's what business people do.'

The Federation of Small Businesses (FSB) soon came out of the traps to put the boot in, too. Represented by National Chairman John Wright, the FSB said they were 'extremely disappointed by the comments made recently by Lord Sugar about small firms. Despite being appointed by the Government to champion business in the UK, Lord Sugar seems to have no grasp of the hard work small businesses do and the role they play in employing six in ten of the country's private sector workforce and contributing to more than half of UK GDP. Lord Sugar appears to have let his TV personality from *The Apprentice* take over and the language he has used to describe this country's small business owners is hardly appropriate given his current role. Members of the FSB have been in touch to complain about Lord Sugar's recent performances around the country and we have to call that he resign from his position. We urge the Prime Minister to appoint someone with a greater understanding of, and more empathy for, the small business sector.'

Sugar later responded, saying: 'All I can say to the Federation of Small Businesses is they need to be careful not to be too depressing.'

All the same, the FSB statement had echoes in Parliament where Shadow Commons Leader Sir George Young asked Commons Leader Harriet Harman whether it was time for Sugar to be shown the door. In turning Sugar's television catchphrase against him, Young might have thought that he was being original, but plenty have done the same trick before. 'With the FSB calling for Lord Sugar to go, do you think he still has the confidence of the companies that he is supposedly meant to be representing?' he asked. 'Or is it time to say "You're fired"?' Harman rather dodged the question but did later tell Conservative MP Andrew Mackay that she would look into Sugar's comments.

Conservative MP David Willetts put the boot in too. Willetts asked Rosie Winterton, the Minister for the Department for Business, Innovation and Skills: 'If the Minister is so keen on apprenticeships, will he explain to the House why, in the leaked document that I have before me, he proposes cuts to the funding of apprenticeships and why he is doing so little to help apprentices who are losing their jobs during the recession? Why does he not adopt our policy of a clearing house to help apprentices who lose their jobs to find new employers? If he will not do that, why does he not ask Lord Sugar to take that on? That might be a better use of Lord Sugar's time than denouncing Britain's hard-working small businesses which is all that he seems to do at the moment. Or is it a case of "Lord Sugar, you're fired"?'

Fellow Tory MP John Howell then followed up: 'Picking up the point that my Honourable Friend [Willetts] made, I wonder whether the Minister agrees with her new noble friend Lord Sugar, the Prime Minister's Enterprise Tsar, who said that those small businesses that are trying to seek credit are merely moaners and living in Disneyland?'

Winterton replied that it was 'not my understanding of what Lord Sugar said'.

Shadow Business Secretary Ken Clarke also weighed in. 'At a time when 51 companies are going bust every day in this country and when, as we said a few moments ago, the credit position for small businesses is very difficult, does the Minister agree with Lord Sugar, the Small Business Tsar, that struggling small businessmen are moaners and living in Disneyland, which he undoubtedly said?' asked Clarke. 'Is it not time for the department's senior minister in the House of Commons to apologise on behalf of the Government for what was said? Otherwise, it will appear that they are indifferent to, and out of tune with, the problems of entrepreneurs up and down the country who are trying to save their businesses and other people's jobs.'

It was not only in the Commons that Lord Sugar came under fire for his frank approach to public events. If ever he wanted a crash course in the extra responsibility that public life gives a man, here it was, for questions were also asked in the House of Lords as the row rumbled on. Those watching might have wondered whether the Government was comfortable being associated with some of what Sugar had said. On 12 November, Lord Davies was repeatedly pressed as to whether Sugar had spoken with the authority of the Government. Davies eventually replied, unequivocally, that he did.

The exchange started when Lord Hunt of Wirral – for the Conservatives – told peers: 'It has been recently reported that Lord Sugar described struggling businessmen as moaners and many people did rapidly conclude that the First Secretary Lord Mandelson should just summon him and say: "You're fired."' (That old chestnut again.) 'On inquiring with Lord Sugar last night he said his remarks had been misreported, adding there was a recording of them which I hope he might place in the House of Lords library to clear this matter up once and for all.' He then asked Lord Davies, 'Would you clarify whether Lord Sugar is accountable to this House and whether when he speaks on enterprise matters he speaks with the full authority of the Government?'

Lord Davies did his best to paper over the issue, saying that, 'with Lord Sugar you will get sugar and spice.' He added: 'He uses colourful language and he uses it forcibly. I see him regularly and he is doing a good job.'

The peers were not assuaged, only scenting further blood in Davies' vagueness. Lord Razzall of the Liberal Democrats turned to reported remarks Sugar had made about female employees. 'I quote him: "They think to themselves she's young, she's attractive, what's going to happen when she gets a boyfriend?" Is that your opinion? Does Lord Sugar speak for the Government on this issue?'

Lord Davies again avoided a direct answer and said instead that Lord Sugar employed a number of women in high-profile positions. By this point his equivocal stance was beginning to be damaging for Sugar's authority. Surely, observers felt, he could not avoid the question much longer. The exchange was becoming reminiscent of the infamous interview Jeremy Paxman conducted with Michael Howard on *Newsnight*, when Paxman repeatedly asked Howard the same question.

The assembled peers were being every bit as persistent as Paxman had been.

Tory former minister Lord Ferrers demanded: 'When Lord Sugar speaks, does he speak with the authority of the Government?'

Lord Davies replied again without directly addressing the question. 'He is accountable to me. I see him on a consistent basis. He is working as an adviser not a policy maker.'

That was not going to make anyone give up the hunt for a 'yes' or 'no' answer.

Conservative ex-Cabinet minister Lord Tebbit asked, 'Does he speak with the authority of the Government or not?'

Could this finally be the moment where an answer emerged? Not quite, it turned out. This time, Lord Davies replied: 'I've answered it. He is accountable to me, I'm a minister. He is not a policy maker, he is an adviser.'

Hats off to Liberal Democrat Lord Dykes, then. He finally got a straight answer when he asked: 'Does he speak with the authority of the Government?'

To the relief of many watching, Lord Davies replied: 'Yes.'

Davies may have – very belatedly – supported Sugar as he came under fire in the Lords, but out in the real world he was still polarising opinion in the wake of his fiery comments. Indeed, some of the very people he had hoped to inspire and represent in his new role were less than impressed with what they had heard. David

Foreman of glass installation specialist Forefit Structural Glass Solutions said, 'His comments didn't seem to be very helpful – they go against the people he's supposed to be representing.'

Diane Ellis of PR firm Peter Troy The Publicist said, 'He should be out there doing something with the banks. He's forgotten what it's like for small businesses.'

Jo Hand of Middlesbrough's Jo Hand Recruitment said many modern-day staff would not respond well to the serial entrepreneur's 'autocratic and old-fashioned' management style. Even then, though, she had an underlying admiration for him. 'In a lot of modern organisations he could be seen as quite offensive – but he does often talk a lot of sense.'

It had been a bruising aftermath to his speeches and the pain was not to subside easily. The following month, Sugar again defended himself. 'Brrr, yeah, well, if you believe what was written, they would have a point,' he told a *Sunday Times* interviewer. 'It was a distorted report in which I was quoted out of context,' he said. He set a task – not an *Apprentice*-style one, mind – to the interviewer, to try and prove that he had been quoted unfairly. 'The fact was,' says Sugar, 'that wasn't what I said. I took the precaution of recording the whole seminar for this very reason. I'll play you the clip, the actual thing, and then after that, I'd like you to take your time, drink some coffee and read that article. And you tell me whether, you know, you think that's fair representation.' Sugar was clearly still fuming from the incident and its fall-out.

The *Sunday Times* interviewer admits to feeling intimidated just six questions into the interview, describing Sugar's style as 'aggressive and weapons-grade charmless'. When she read out the quotes Goldberg made after the event, Sugar slapped her down. 'But you see, dare I suggest you're reading from a newspaper?' he said. 'How do you know he said that?' When she attempted to press on with her point, he shouted, 'His reaction is wrong! It's as simple as that. I'm a bit concerned that you are taking what you choose to read in the newspaper as fact.'

He seemed to have been shaken by the controversy. 'Too much negative stuff is really unhelpful,' he said. 'I may decide that this is simply not worth it, when you're giving your time free of charge for no agenda. What am I going to get out of it? I'm not getting paid. I've not got my titles for the sake of a badge.' However, such wobbling seemed to be a short-term affair. 'I am the man on this subject,' he said proudly, almost defiantly. 'I don't think anyone else can give the depth of advice and experience I have had over the years.'

Of suggestions that, following the controversy, he intended to resign, he said, 'I have made a commitment to help support small businesses and I have no intention of going back on my word. Based on the letters of support I receive from those who have attended my seminars, the feedback has all been very positive, and that's what counts.'

So it was that he moved on to the aforementioned events, at Manchester Hilton and East Midlands Conference Centre. Both were thrillers, full of fantastic moments of trademark Sugar honesty. 'If people are in business, they are in business because they don't want to work for someone else, because they think they have a skill,' Lord Sugar told the audience in Nottingham. 'They think they have a talent or something extra about them that makes them special. People seem to think they are owed something by the Government or their bank. You have to sort these things out yourself. People are in business, they can take advantage of things like Business Link and banks.'

He went on to answer questions from people from a range of different businesses, from customer service trainers to furniture manufacturers. One such entrepreneur asked Sugar for advice on how to dodge the increasing tightness of compliance rules. 'I looked at compliance like the Grand National – lots of hurdles,' said Sugar. 'In my business, which I started 40 years ago, there were no laws about electrical safety. Effectively you could make something and kill yourself with it. As time went on we had to change. Customers said to me, "We won't buy your stuff unless it has a stamp on it." Imagine yourself as a baseball bat. Every time someone puts something in your way, whack it out of the way.' It was vivid, powerful advice. Inspiring, too, and always honest. He concluded: 'You and me are not going to change this compliance system. We are in the European Community and we are stuffed with the stuff they send over to us. It's as simple as that.'

On and on the questions came. A woman who made shoes designed to be worn by women after a night in heels was advised to approach one of the leading supermarkets for their small business scheme. A man who wanted to develop social networking schemes for football clubs got candid and succinct advice from Sugar, who still looks back with horror at his own experience in the game: don't bother. 'They are just not interested unless there is money in it for them. Don't go to football clubs.'

At the end of the event, Sugar was delighted at the response to his honest approach. He said: 'I think it went well. I was very pleased with the kind of questions. That's exactly what I wanted to do with people, to speak in particular about their business rather than listen to a lot of moaning. I'm there to give people ideas.' He would have been disappointed that a handful of reports of the event focused on the exchange with the cake-making woman rather than the plentiful positivity that happened. The same would happen at the Manchester event.

However, there was plenty of valuable, appreciated advice dished out by him at the event, leading to the *Manchester Evening News*'s headline praising Sugar for his SWEET ADVICE FOR BUSINESS BOSSES. Questions were thrown at him by the audience and his words were priceless. One audience member asked for advice after a customer enforced payment terms where bills would not be settled until 120 days after the month end. Lord Sugar said: 'If you are powerful enough you can tell them to "stick it". If not, you will have to live with it and maybe put your prices up a bit.'

Then Cheshire cosmetics manufacturer Linda Hutchinson asked Lord Sugar how best to get her products into high street stores. 'My suggestion is: don't aim at getting your products in Boots straight away. You need to build your business through smaller boutique retailers.'

All the same, his quote about 15 per cent of small businesses was the one that continued to grab attention. Lord Sugar's spokesperson stepped in afterwards to insist that Sugar was not claiming that only 15 per cent of all small businesses were worth lending money to, but was referring to the proportion of those that complained they had been refused loans which he felt had cause to 'moan'. The spokesperson also denied Sugar had attacked the Government, saying people's unreasonable expectations were due to misunderstanding what ministers were saying. All the same, he had ruffled feathers galore during his speech – and he wouldn't have had it any other way.

A representative of a firm that needed to get more Government contracts asked Lord Sugar how a smaller business such as his could grab those valuable contracts. 'It is unfair, but sometimes larger, more established companies are getting the business,' said Sugar. 'That is because the public sector decision makers are salary people. Sometimes the decisions they make are based on protecting their jobs. You need to get the first contract, which might mean giving more time and effort than what you get out of it. That will give them the confidence and you have got your way in.' His conclusion was upbeat and succinct. 'Business is bad out there but the good news is that it will come back.'

Lord Sugar came back himself. In November 2009 he returned to the speaking trail when he addressed 800 school and college students at an event that was part of Global Entrepreneurship Week. 'The way forward for British business is in your hands, not in the hands of some old fart like me,' he told them. Lord Sugar added that they should aim to be self-sufficient if they wanted to make it to the top. 'In 1966 I took £100 from my post office savings, bought a Minivan for £50, paid £8 insurance and with the balance bought stuff to sell. It was my greatest investment. In the first week I earned three times what I earned the previous week working for someone else.'

He also appeared at the British Library before a packed audience. Any expectation that he would soften up his views about bank loans were cast aside. 'I have seen some examples of some hopeless cases that no one in this room would lend a penny, let alone me,' he told the audience of entrepreneurs.

One journalist present, Jonathan Guthrie of the *Financial Times*, gave an assessment of the proceedings when he corrected his own previous description that Sugar was 'lecturing' the audience. 'Did I say lecturing?' he asked. 'Haranguing, more like. Tearing off a strip, even.' Guthrie also described the host of the evening, *Real Business* magazine's editor Matthew Rock, as wearing 'the expression of a guppy that finds itself sharing a tank with a piranha'. Elsewhere, Rock himself confirmed his discomfort, writing: 'Apart from getting three sub-five-year-old kids to bed on time, my toughest gig this week was compering the formidable Lord Sugar.'

It was certainly direct stuff. When one audience member told Sugar that he had managed to make technical progress in an industry about which he previously knew nothing, Sugar was dismissive – comically so. 'You must be Tommy Cooper,' he snapped. 'I do not believe you for a moment.' The tycoon added: 'Don't tell me that you come up with a cream to make the ladies' faces all smooth, but previous to that you was [sic] planting daffodils.'

Another audience member asked Sugar about the merits or otherwise of business and enterprise education. 'If you stuffed me in a room with a piano teacher for long enough, I would be able to bang out three choruses of *Roll Out The Barrel*,' he said. 'But could I ever play as a concert pianist in the Royal Albert Hall? Not in a million years.' Later someone tried to turn the conversation round to *The Apprentice*. 'We're not here to discuss that,' was Sugar's curt response. That told them. It was a performance that made Sugar on that show seem tame and retiring in comparison.

Sugar's autumnal speaking engagements of 2009 had been eyebrow-raising affairs indeed. Would he tone down his honesty in the face of his political appointment? The answer was a resounding "no". Sugar had again shown that he is never intimidated.

The shyness – which had been apparent in his earlier years in business – is long gone. Put him on a stage now in front of any kind of audience and he will be confident and even downright prickly. Any audience member who thinks they can get the better of him on the night should beware. They have no chance. As Guthrie commented: 'It was a case of 200 against one. The 200 were badly outnumbered.' They also benefitted, though, from Sugar's advice. Just because he was honest did not mean his words lacked tough love and wisdom. Within weeks, students at the University of Nottingham were being invited by Lord Davies to come for tea in London with himself and Lord Sugar.

To scholars of Sugar's life story, this straight-talking style combined with a kind underbelly came as little surprise. Sugar famously dislikes dishonesty. 'I don't like liars. I don't like cheats. I don't like schmoozers. I don't like a**********s,' was the line famously delivered by Sugar during the opening titles of *The Apprentice*. One wag commented that it sounded as if he was reading a restaurant menu. Still, love him or loathe him, nobody could accuse him of being anything less than honest on the show. Sometimes painfully so. He is a businessman and personality who believes that honesty is always the best policy. Not only does this truthfulness manifest itself in his utterances, but also in the way he conducts his business affairs.

Despite the razor-sharp attention of numerous rivals and the world media, despite endless scrutiny by those cynics who would love to do down his achievements, Sugar has never been exposed for any corruption or wrong-doing. True, a few of his ventures have been less than successful, but those moments are few and far between and evidence merely that, like everyone else, Sugar wins some and loses some. However, he always competes with honesty and integrity.

He was, as we shall see, once asked if there was a Sugar brand. His response was amusing and dismissive, but if there is a word that many would associate with such a brand it is honesty. Since the first days of his life, when his mother Fay recalls him in the hospital acting 'like a boss overriding everyone – he made such a lot of noise,' he has never been short of an opinion.

His dislike of schmoozing continues to this day, finding it insincere and therefore lacking in honesty. However, he recognises that it is a part of the business world. While preferring not to indulge in it himself, he does allow others to do it on behalf of his companies. 'I was told in my younger days that this is what you do, so I did wine and dine – it was dull and insincere,' said Sugar at an event at the Union of Brunel Students. 'Younger people have to do it for me now as I don't have the patience! Entertaining is now a big industry. It drives things like corporate hospitality at race days and football. It is now a deliberately prepared corporate expense. That's how it is in business, people are used to the jollies. Take them away and people might leave.'

He has actually become a benchmark for straight-talking in the business world. When a senior colleague of HSBC chief executive Michael Geoghegan wanted to describe the banker's style, he said: 'He's like Alan Sugar – he talks a load of macho business bollocks and then, after listening to him for 45 minutes, you start to tune in and realise he's pretty sharp.'

Cross swords with Sugar at your peril. When a city analyst described him – bizarrely – as a cross between a Trappist monk and the Muslim prophet Mohammed, Sugar was effortless and direct in his response. 'There should be some professional exam for these analysts. Most of the time they talk through their backsides.'

Even when he is promoting his own products, Sugar arrives straight at the point. When launching the new Amstrad PC1512 computer model in the 1980s, he gave it a true down-to-earth pitch. 'I see it as a real home computer where Father can bring work home from the office on a floppy disc, put it in his machine and work on it on his own desk, before taking it back with him into his office in the morning,' he said to a thousand assembled journalists at the Queen Elizabeth Conference Centre in London. 'At the same time "Sonny Jim" can use it to play *Space Invaders* if he wants.'

He also had a rather cheeky side to the launch, hinting at the costliness of the rival IBM computer models. A huge pair of red lips was shown on a giant screen. The lips explained what the many benefits of the Amstrad PC1512 were. Then the eight models that formed the PC1512 range were unveiled. The accompanying television advertisement said: 'Compatible with you-know-who. Priced as only we know how.'

It's easy to dish out honesty, but Sugar can also face the flack that sometimes comes as a result. Amstrad was the new kid on the computer block and while Sugar was unafraid to ruffle the feathers of the big boys already in that market, he knew that this would lead to some unpleasant remarks being thrown his way. Ever the thick-skinned man, however, he could face the music. Indeed, in one of his chairman's statements during the 1980s he almost welcomed the stir that Amstrad had caused in the computer world. 'The Amstrad effect of course rocked the boat,' he said, 'the resultant factor being critical comments of the product, with which I am sure all and sundry are familiar. I think Pythagoras and Columbus had the same problem when they announced the world was round.'

To be clear, he is not mindlessly dismissive of rivals and also often speaks favourably of others in the computer industry, including Microsoft founder Bill Gates. 'You can only admire him for his vision that software was going to drive the computer industry,' he said. 'When we were the kingpins of the computer business in the UK and Europe, he came to my home and sat there discussing business. I'm not saying that we're bosom buddies and that we call each other up all the time but if you mentioned my name I'm sure that he would know me.'

There is a Yiddish proverb that says: 'A half truth is a whole lie.' Sugar certainly strives to conduct himself with the truth, the whole truth and nothing but the truth. There has always been a sense of fair play at the heart of Britain and part of that quality is honesty. To some commentators, it might at first seem to be a contradictory pairing: fairness and honesty. Certainly if the latter quality is little more than rudeness then the contrast would be clear to all. However, a true gentleman can combine the two effortlessly, and Lord Sugar would fall into that category. This is not a recent trend. Lord Sugar's outspoken nature was, to those who subscribe to such beliefs, possibly secured at birth, given the star-sign he was born under. Arians are often honest and forthright. Some astrologers say those born under the sign of the ram frequently lack tact. Certainly those who have faced his direct verdicts and jabbing finger in the boardroom of *The Apprentice* will agree that Sugar has *both* honesty and forthrightness in spades.

Indeed, honesty and business have all too often gone together in a harsh manner. In the rough and tumble of business, it was believed that the only honesty with any currency was the fist slamming down on the table, accompanied by the abusive barking of another order. 'Honesty is never seen sitting astride the fence,' goes the saying. Have you ever seen Sugar sitting on the fence on *The Apprentice*? Never. However, when television and business went head-to-head with the dawn of *The Apprentice*, there was a danger that the honesty on show would go beyond anything acceptable, bringing together, as it did, two notoriously brusque worlds.

Since the turn of the century reality TV has become a format in which blunt speaking is the order of the day. From 2000 when *Popstars* judge Nigel Lythgoe became Nasty Nigel thanks to his direct verdicts at auditions, the die was cast. Indeed, one could argue that the 21st-century brutality of reality television is merely following on from – and exaggerating – the to-the-point verdicts given by the likes of Mickie Most on ITV's *New Faces*, which was first broadcast in 1973. The most celebrated proponent of this trend is Simon Cowell, who loved to watch Most back in the 1970s. Music executive Cowell – who had declined an invitation to be the 'nasty' judge on *Popstars* – became infamous overnight when he offered withering judgements to contestants on 2001's ITV show *Pop Idol*. Cowell – who went on to judge on *American Idol*, *The X Factor* and *Britain's Got Talent* – became more famous than the shows' winners, thanks to his straight talking. International fame and considerable fortune came his way, too.

The same happened for Anne Robinson, whose rudeness to contestants on *The Weakest Link* turned her from an averagely famous British television personality to an American superstar. No matter that Cowell is famously unimpressed with Robinson: she had followed his example and cackled all the way to the bank. A trend had been started and widely noted: a blunt character on television earned millions of viewers for the programme and enormous advantage for the character concerned.

This trend then transferred to business-based reality shows, such as *Dragon's Den* and *The Apprentice*. Rightly so. No candidate would learn anything on the latter show if they were soft-soaped by the man at the head of the table. There is no room in business for soft, disingenuous talk. Reportedly, this is why Virgin tycoon Richard Branson was not given the role on *The Apprentice*. His smiling, gentle public persona might be admirable and agreeable generally, but it would not do the job in the cut and thrust of the boardroom bollocking sessions which were to be a gripping part of the television show. Donald Trump had – on the original American version of the show – laid down the marker for *The Apprentice* franchise. An abrupt, roaring voice in the boardroom was the only way to make the show authentic and entertaining. Who in Britain could possibly replicate that? Well, there was one obvious candidate...

The programme makers duly turned to Lord Sugar. 'I'm sure they knocked on all the usual suspects' doors before they got to me, but while some businessmen may be clever and bright, they can dry up in front of a camera,' he said. 'I'd been on so many money programmes and faced the cameras constantly when I was chairman of Tottenham Hotspur, and I made it clear that I thought *The Apprentice* was something I could do.'

At last, the torments of Tottenham (of which more later) were paying dividends for Sugar. He was keen to sign up to the show. 'I really wanted to do it,' he said. 'I think it's a great concept. It also falls in line with the enterprise work I have been doing with the Government … to promote business. What most people don't realise is that business isn't about the big corporations. It's about "Harry", who's got ten blokes who work for him at the garage round the corner. We have got to encourage young people to be more enterprising.' With his part on *The Apprentice*, he felt, he could do just that. '*The Apprentice* is a 12-week crash course in business survival techniques. Grounded in commercial reality, it is not for the faint-hearted,' he said. 'It doesn't claim to turn everyone into an entrepreneur.'

He was keen and so were the production team. With his television experience and self-confidence, Sugar seemed the ideal choice for the producers of *The Apprentice*. The man who had made a fortune from television during his work on the launch of BSkyB with

Rupert Murdoch would now move in front of the camera to establish a new direction in his career. It was a long way from the nervous days as he started his business career when those closest to him noted how painfully shy he could be if called upon to speak in public.

What had caused this shyness in Sugar? Perhaps it was due to the big age difference between himself and his nearest siblings – 12 years between him and twins David and Daphne. He was never particularly outgoing in his childhood either. Due to the age gap, he was in a sense an only child. Even on his first day at school he showed how shy and homely he was. Having been dropped off at the beginning of the day, Sugar was back home at 11am having walked out of the school during mid-morning break. Who could have predicted then not just the riches, but also the fame ahead for this meek boy? Who would have expected him to make himself an internationally famous figure on television, jabbing his fingers at people as he gave them a harsh dressing-down?

By the time he took up the job, though, he had gained plenty of experience of public speaking, television work and the key part of *The Apprentice* role – firing people. Not in an overly aggressive way, however. 'I've very rarely had to violently sack someone,' he explained. 'Usually it's an accumulation of events and you end up saying "I'm sorry. I'm going to have to let you go." I don't enjoy doing it, but if it has to be done, it has to be done.'

It was, as much as anything else, Sugar's honesty that landed him the role on *The Apprentice*. A man more than capable of shooting from the hip, he was just what the producers ordered. He delivers what is required so effortlessly because for him honest talking is not something to be contrived for the cameras: it is how he lives his life.

'The beauty of the show is that there's no act whatsoever,' he said. 'It's for real.' However, even when at his most outspoken on *The Apprentice*, Lord Sugar never descends into anything genuinely unpleasant or bullying on screen. How very different it is across the Atlantic, where *The Apprentice* franchise was born.

In 2006, Donald Trump became involved in a prolonged public war of words with US media personality Rosie O'Donnell. The slanging match became increasingly personal and bitter, with both casting professional and personal aspersions against one another. Naturally, the media loved the battle between two of Manhattan's biggest personalities, but the words became more and more harsh, with Trump describing O'Donnell as 'a total degenerate'. Perhaps the lowest blow came when Trump, referring to O'Donnell's public admission that she suffered from depression, suggested on the *Entertainment Tonight* show that if she wished to stop being depressed she should stop looking in the mirror. This was unsettling to watch for many observers. It is unimaginable that Sugar would resort to such a tactic, on or off screen. Compared to Trump, Sugar is sweetness itself.

In his book *Think Big and Kick Ass!* Trump recounts the entire story of his feud with O'Donnell, stating that there was nothing wrong with what he said and using the episode as an example of the power of revenge. O'Donnell, he points out, ceased criticising him once she realised he would hit back harder. The effectiveness of his conduct is not the main question – the real question is did he go too far in his criticism of her? A line had surely been crossed.

Lord Sugar's brand of honesty is potent and well known, but he would never allow it to spill into such a nasty public feud, least of all with an unhappy woman. His particular sense of dignity and personal code of ethics would never allow it. That said, he did permit himself a dig at Trump. He was being filmed in a speedboat on the River Thames for some opening shots of *The Apprentice*. Between takes he turned to the camera crew and joked that Trump would be unable to appear in a similar set-up, because his comb-over would be blown off his head.

Despite their differences, Trump praises Sugar's performances on *The Apprentice* and says that he was personally involved in the decision to hire him. 'He does a good job over there,' Trump told *Seven* magazine. 'I chose him with [British TV producer] Mark Burnett. We have tried this format in lots of countries with different entrepreneurs and Alan has done it best.'

Trump was not so impressed, however, with Richard Branson's business show. 'When my show became a success I had all these people trying to copy it,' he said. 'I really like Richard, even though he tried to copy my show and failed. His show bombed whereas mine was the number one rated. *The Apprentice* has just been renewed for two more years.'

Sugar's place on the UK show may have the seal of approval from his US equivalent, but not all is rosy with the American *Apprentice* in the eyes of Lord Sugar. He feels that, when it comes to *The Apprentice*, less is definitely more. The American series suffered a dramatic dip in viewers from 20 million for the first series to just eight million by the time of series six. Sugar, ever the canny observer, put his finger on where things went wrong in typically blunt mode. 'In my opinion, the mistake that the Americans made was, instead of making it an annual event, they ran three series back to back in a 13-month period,' he said. 'People got sick and tired of it and the pressure on the production people to come up with credible tasks was immense. Tasks started to slip and the candidates started to slip and what was left was a pile of rubbish.'

Sugar has insisted that he won't make the same mistake with the UK version. 'What we have here is an annual event. There's longevity in the programme simply because the audience is looking forward to it again,' he said. Indeed it is, with each new instalment feverishly anticipated and discussed. The internet forums, water-coolers and bus stops of Britain can scarcely get enough of Sugar's show. He feels fully vindicated in his decision to go on a show he feels is not just great entertainment but also a force for good. 'I really think it opens a window into the business world, and that's why I do it,' he says forcefully. 'I know that top businessmen profess to think it's all a bit of a joke, but while they're sitting there calling the candidates a bunch of pr****, they're all glued to the programme. But I also know for an undisputed fact that kids from 11-15 are the biggest audience. They love it and learn from it.'

Sugar's trademark boardroom hard-talk might have followed on from the legacy of Cowell and Robinson, but he has duly set one of his own, transferring his honest style to others in the television sphere. The panel on the BBC business pitching show *Dragons' Den* has become more and more outspoken as time has gone on. Dragon Peter Jones is perhaps the most obvious example. Having always been a straight-talker during the show, the telecommunications mogul seems to have become more exasperated by, and rude towards, the pitching would-be entrepreneurs. As early as the first series he berated fellow Dragon Duncan Bannatyne for undercutting him on a deal. 'You've just put a guy on the bloody edge here and you've just completely been a sly little shit,' he told the Scot. However, his sharp tongue was soon being turned against the contestants. He routinely rolls his eyes before the contestants have even finished their pitches and is often robust and seemingly bad-mannered in his subsequent questioning of them.

Could it be that Jones is eyeing a possible future place on Sugar's boardroom chair? Rumours that Sugar will be replaced have risen in the past. In December 2006, newspapers confidently predicted that he was on his way out, quoting unnamed 'sources' to this effect. 'There's a growing number of people at the BBC who don't think Alan Sugar is the right man for the job any more,' said the BBC source. 'It's also true that Sir Alan only did the third series on certain conditions. We don't really even know if he'd do a fourth. *The Apprentice* is a great show because you don't know what's going to happen next. It's more about the format than the boss and we don't want to lose its freshness.'

It was suggested by the same source that Duncan Bannatyne had been lined up to join the show. 'We also know from *Dragons' Den* that Duncan Bannatyne can perform. All the Dragons have big egos and all of them would probably want to do it, but Duncan has a high enough profile that he could realistically carry a proper show.'

The Scot confirmed he would be interested, saying: 'If ever Alan Sugar retires and they were looking for someone else, I'd be more than happy to do it.'

Sugar's quality of honesty has also been turned against his *Apprentice* show. Speaking in 2008, after candidate

Lee McQueen had been hired as the new apprentice, despite being caught lying on his CV, Jones was scathing. 'I'm a fan of Sir Alan, but the last series was a bit fictional,' he said. 'The idea of recruiting anyone who lied on their CV just isn't credible. It's turning into an entertaining *Big Brother*-type show rather than a programme about business reality.'

A few months later Jones turned his wrath from the show to Sugar himself, suggesting he should retire and allow Jones to take his place. 'I don't know how old Sir Alan is, but he must be 70 or 75 at least,' he said, adding that at 6ft 7in, he would not need the booster seat 5ft 6in Sugar has been rumoured to require. It was a story that would have been embarrassing to Sugar – had there been any serious proof of it.

The London *Evening Standard* was the first to carry this allegation, with photographs suggesting the chair sits on a raised platform. The newspaper quoted an *Apprentice* contestant as saying: 'I did notice when he got on his chair he did do a sort of little jump to get on it.' Virgin Radio then picked up the story.

An *Apprentice* spokesperson denied that the seat is raised for any reasons of vanity. 'Being a swivel chair, there is a wooden frame, bolted to the floor, into which the five wheels are sunk – to anchor it for camera positions,' he said.

Sugar himself was unsurprisingly robust in his denial of the booster seat allegations. 'That's a load of rubbish,' he said. 'The chair is fixed to stop it moving backwards and forwards, while allowing me to swing to the left and the right. Anyone who watches the programme will know that I stand next to Nick [Hewer] and Margaret [Mountford] and the candidates, and I'm seen getting out of the car thousands of times. It's a total joke. It's there to secure the four wheels to stop it moving backwards and forwards. It's a total joke.'

It was a convincing answer, but it was not enough to convince all observers. Some are always delighted to find a weak spot in a successful person, all the better to ease their own envy and disappointment with their own lot in life.

The sniping from the rival business show continued. Jones's *Den* co-star Theo Paphitis echoed his co-star's sentiments. He said: 'I used to watch *The Apprentice*, but it's become *Big Brother*. They all live in a house together and are given tasks – where do you recognise that? I don't think it's challenging anymore… I like Alan Sugar. I think he's fabulous. But the whole format and the things that the contestants do – it's not a million miles away from what happens in *Big Brother*, which isn't the most intellectually stimulating programme.'

Bannatyne, too, was critical of Sugar. In the wake of Lee McQueen missing his first day at work as Sugar's apprentice, he was dismissive of Sugar's decision to hire him. 'That's what happens when you employ a liar,' Bannatyne is quoted by the *Mirror* as saying. 'I'm so angry that Alan Sugar sent that message out to the country. "If you want a job, kids, lie on your CV." I'm disgusted.' The Scot has often been keen to take the high ground on all manner of issues, and has told more than one *Dragons' Den* pitcher that he hopes their venture will fail due to his moral issues with the product they have created.

Sugar has largely kept quiet in response to the jibes of Bannatyne and his cohorts, but he is no shrinking violet and not averse to a public spat when the mood takes him. In the spring of 2008 he and former tabloid newspaper editor Piers Morgan had a glorious public row over the popularity of their respective shows – *The Apprentice* and *Britain's Got Talent* – as they went head-to-head in the ratings battle and for a prestigious BAFTA.

Morgan has long been a controversial figure, not least since he was sacked from the *Daily Mirror* newspaper over printing faked photographs that purported to show British troops torturing Iraqi prisoners. He has since built himself a successful television career, but he still manages to be involved in arguments on a regular basis. Sugar claimed that if *Britain's Got Talent* won, it would not be down to Morgan's presence on the show's panel. 'It will be thanks to Simon Cowell, the organ grinder, rather than his monkey, Piers Morgan,' he said. Ouch!

But Morgan has the hide of an elephant and gave as good as he got. 'Being called a monkey by Sir Alan is like being called fat by Sir Nicholas Soames,' he roared. 'Sugar looks more like a monkey to me than anyone. But I take these insults in the good spirit they are intended.

'*Britain's Got Talent* has been hitting about 11.5 million while *The Apprentice* has about 8.5 million viewers,' he told the *Daily Star*. 'I loved it the other day when Sir Alan sent me a text comparing himself to a maggot because he says his show is going to slowly catch up and overtake us in the ratings war. I decided to look the definition of maggot up in the dictionary and I have to say I agree with his description of himself. A maggot is described as like "a larva often found in decaying, dying matter". In American dictionaries they call a maggot a "revolting human being". I would probably agree with that also.' Well, that was certainly to the point.

As it was, after all that rowing, neither *The Apprentice* nor *Britain's Got Talent* won the BAFTA, which instead went to BBC Three comedy show *Gavin and Stacey*. Sugar was most unimpressed. He was reportedly overheard on the phone saying: 'Gavin and what?'

Morgan, too, was nonplussed. 'I didn't even know there was a BBC Three,' he groaned.

That said, their public battle had been very entertaining. While there had undoubtedly been some element of pantomime to the argument, Morgan does not seem to be a major fan of Sugar. He might have won the American series of *Celebrity Apprentice*, but he did not fare so well on the British equivalent when he came face-to-face with Sugar. He was the candidate Sugar chose to fire when his team finished runners-up on the 2007 edition of *Comic Relief Does The Apprentice*.

Fortunately, the spat was over quickly, certainly compared to Morgan's ongoing – and some would say tiresome – rows with *Private Eye* editor Ian Hislop and broadcaster Jeremy Clarkson.

Sugar has a humorous side when it comes to battles with other celebs that are little more than a bit of fun. In October 2009 he came fourth in a poll asking who was the greatest leader of all time. Speaking to the press, he joked about those he had finished in front of. 'I beat Moses,' he said. 'I don't know what's better – that or beating Simon Cowell!'

The Youth of Today survey, which was commissioned by the Prince's Trust and polled more than a thousand young people, named Martin Luther King as the greatest leader, with Barack Obama the runner-up. According to the survey, 70 per cent of teenagers say they are more likely be inspired by someone they know than by a celebrity, a statistic which runs against the received wisdom that today's youth are obsessed with fame and the famous. Adam Nichols, from The Youth of Today, said: 'People think that youth today only aspire to be like celebrities, but they're wrong. This campaign will give young people more inspiration closer to home.' It also showed that even as he enters old age, Sugar continues to be relevant and to appeal to all ages.

Sugar's honesty is nothing new or peculiar to his work on *The Apprentice*. It is the way he has lived his life and career since as long as anyone close to him can remember.

Right from the start of his business journey, the one that would take him to the top of the tree, he has been on a mission. 'I was ... angry and probably a bit arrogant,' he recalled of the early days. 'I was sick of putting money in other people's pockets when I knew I could earn more on my own.' No longer did he want to work in a stuffy civil service office or sell shoes. Nor was he inclined to follow his father's lifetime of 'playing the safe game', though he was grateful to and loving of his father. He just felt they were different.

'I had seen [him] work hard all his life, putting the family first and playing the safe game in order to take care of us.' Sugar felt that in a highly important respect, he differed from his father, both in circumstances and make-up. 'I was at the point when I had no responsibilities – and I knew I didn't have his temperament – I would never be able to stay the course working for someone else.'

Perhaps it was that anger, that yearning to break the mould he felt his family had set for him, that informed Sugar's direct, to-the-point working modus operandi. With Sugar what you see is what you get. As far back as the 1970s when he began his empire, he faced prejudice because of his background and more. For instance, as an electrical trade magazine journalist recalled of those years, even Sugar's appearance was an issue. 'Beards weren't very popular in those days and he always looked slightly dishevelled,' recalled Arthur Ord-Hume. A simple five-minute shave could have dealt with this but

Sugar was not about to compromise his appearance for anyone. He was comfortable wearing a beard and the rest of the world would have to just deal with it.

It is interesting that such an ambitious man was willing to make so many sacrifices to get to the top but was stubbornly not prepared to make changes that he felt would be untrue to himself. So he went about his business looking exactly the way he wanted, and was quickly making a reputation for himself as a straight-talker with no time for insincere niceties. For instance, when he was asked what his P/E (price-to-earnings) ratios were, he thought of physical education (PE) and replied: 'Twenty press-ups every morning.'

Soon he was taking such sentiments away from stuffy meeting rooms and into a wider arena. In April 1987 he gave the first major public airing of his business methodology. He had long been courted to give a public speech about his professional philosophy but up to this point, he had never accepted any requests. However, when the City University Business School in London invited him he pitched up on the night to deliver a memorable lecture. The audience was 300-strong and any nerves that Sugar might have felt were hard to detect on the night. 'I have had a bellyful of Americans who flit from job to job and exist in large empires as statistics,' he told an audience of captivated students, adding that at some corporate giants, 'the left hand does not know what the right hand is doing.'

That speech became legendary in the story of Sugar's

life. The City University Business School had been visited before by successful figures, but none had been quite as honest and outspoken as Sugar. He warned the budding business people not to be distracted by the attention of 'groupie-type poseurs who wish to be seen with the new blue-eyed boy'. He added that his ambition in life was not to 'be seen daily at Annabel's with Lord and Lady Beseenwith'. Perhaps some of the audience held dreams of working for Amstrad? 'We don't want any corporate wimps,' their guest speaker warned them.

Honest? This was unparalleled truth-speaking from Sugar. His straight talking came to the fore in his speech's mirth-making conclusion. 'Pan Am takes good care of you. Marks & Spencer loves you. IBM says the customer is king,' he said, outlining the companies' key slogans, before turning to his own. 'At Amstrad, we want your money.' This common sense speaking was the stuff that separates the lectures that enliven, inform and motivate audiences from those that bore them rigid.

When he spoke to the Brunel Students Union shortly after his knighthood in 2000, he was equally straight to the point. Asked whether he subsequently regretted not going to university himself, he replied, 'No. I'm brighter than most of the students here.' His chairman's statements in the Amstrad days were similarly direct. Nowadays, with his celebrity status added to the mix, Sugar is a highly sought-after speaker. However, he doesn't come cheap...

The Amstrad office resonated with the sound of

honesty from the start. Malcolm Miller joined the company in 1979 as the company's first marketing executive. He had completed a degree in Business Studies at Central London Polytechnic and worked at Bird's Eye and Unilever. To say he was cut from similar cloth to Sugar would be an understatement. The pair even resembled each other (though Miller was taller and thinner) and had similar mannerisms. In giving him the job, Sugar had warned him that he would need to learn fast. This was no Unilever and he would not be given some of the luxuries he enjoyed there, such as secretarial support. What he was given, however, was a straightforward working environment. Years later, he assessed how important honesty was to Sugar. 'Nothing gets hidden here,' he boasted. 'People are very straight talkers. If you don't like straight talking or you're shocked by being told your idea is crap, then don't come to Amstrad, because we don't pull our punches.'

In doing so, Sugar was becoming an increasingly well-known entrepreneur. As many who have found fame and financial fortune quickly discover, this is a mixed blessing. People from your past – and those claiming to be from your past – emerge to try and get their slice of the action. During the second half of the 1980s, Sugar experienced an increasing amount of unwelcome attention from people who claimed they were old friends from Hackney. 'The school I went to in Hackney must have had 250 million boys in it, because everybody that phones claims to know me, or went to school with me, or knows a brother who's got an uncle who knows an aunt who knows me.' As these calls continued to come in to his office, Sugar felt that definitive action was needed to prevent these timewasters from disrupting his working day.

'The phone does not stop ringing from nine o'clock in the morning to six o'clock at night,' he told David Thomas. 'Honestly, I can't talk to everybody who picks up the phone to me every day. So Frances, my secretary, has got this patter of politely saying to people, "Who are you? Do you really know Mr Sugar?"'

This was a wise way of filtering calls, but Sugar's stock response led to one toe-curling but entertaining slip-up in the year following his City University speech. In May 1988, his secretary told him that a Mr Rupert Murdoch was on the line waiting to speak to him. Sugar is, by his own admission, not great at remembering names. So without even looking up he said, 'I've never heard of him. Tell him to piss off, clear off... I bet he thinks he went to my school.' He added that unless this person called Rupert Murdoch would say what he was calling about, he would not be taking the call.

His secretary returned with the news that 'Mr Murdoch doesn't normally tell people what his business is before speaking to them himself' and that he had consequently rung off.

'But who is he?' asked Sugar.

His secretary replied, 'He owns *The Sun*, *The Times*,

the *Sunday Times*, the *News of the World* and *Today* newspapers.'

Sugar was horrified at his error. 'Oh, my God,' he said. 'Quick, get him back on the line'. As he later explained to Thomas: 'The problem with me is I'm very bad on names and also I'm very bad at reading the newspapers. I'm very unworldly in the sense that outside the electronics and computer industries, I don't know the names of big-shot businessmen. If you asked me who is the chairman of BAT or Shell or British Telecom, I wouldn't know. There are people who go around name-dropping all the time, saying Sir John This or Sir John That and you're supposed to know who they're talking about. I really don't. Sometimes people think I'm lying, but I'm not.'

True, this might not be the best characteristic for a rising star but there is a genuine side to it that one can only admire. Equally, the forthright way he admits to the problem he has with memorising people's names shows a level of self-awareness and openness that is definitely to be respected. It has certainly not held him back in the business world and, as we shall see, he went on to work with spectacular success alongside Rupert Murdoch on a key project.

Like all businessmen, Sugar has had his rough patches when things have not gone his way. But it is in the tough times of business that a man's honesty is truly tested. As the 1980s drew to a close, Amstrad suffered a lot of dark moments. It lost £114 million in sales because it did not have the products to meet the demand. Meanwhile, its foreign subsidiaries began to perform badly too, with the share value collapsing as a result. Sugar now showed that his honesty comes out in bad times and good, when he reacted to all this gloom by painfully and openly analysing what had gone wrong during a legendary meeting at the Amstrad headquarters with the dreaded city analysts. They had arrived stressed after rail problems had delayed their journey, scenting blood in Amstrad's woes. If they expected to find their old adversary in defensive or deceptive mood as a result of his company's dip in fortunes, they were to be surprised.

Sugar told them why pre-tax profits for the six months to the end of 1988 were down 16 per cent to £75.3 million. Getting straight to the point, he declared that he wanted to call the financial year 'the year of disaster'. His advisers had earlier suggested that this was not a sensible term to use, but that did not stop Sugar. His honest, open style was matched by Amstrad's marketing director Malcolm Miller, who sat next to Sugar at the gathering.

'We've been critical of ourselves,' said Miller. 'We've tried to understand what went wrong, so we can decide what to do.'

Sugar turned to the problems that had beset the distribution of computers in West Germany. '1988 was planned to be the first year that Amstrad Germany was to show a major contribution to the group result,' he said. 'I am sorry to say that in the first half this did not go according to plan... we accept in hindsight that this situation was self-inflicted.' Drawing to a rousing climax, Sugar was once more self-searching and honest. 'We made some bad mistakes. I don't really know why so many things went wrong at the one time. But come the new financial year, we will be firing on all cylinders again.'

He had been honest and brilliant throughout the meeting, and the City analysts left impressed. Not that this was enough in itself to go against the harsh realities of business. That same day the share price fell 12 per cent, knocking £57 million off the value of Sugar's personal stake in the company.

The media spread this tale of woe. The American *Wall Street Journal* – generally a fan of Sugar – headlined its story: AMSTRAD TAKES HUMBLING TURN FOR ALAN SUGAR. *The Times* told its readers PROFITS TUMBLE TO £75 MILLION AFTER AMSTRAD "MISTAKES". The story explained, 'Amstrad, the consumer electronics group, saw £125 million wiped off its market capitalisation yesterday after reporting a year-on-year pre-tax profits drop for the first time in its history.'

The news was no better elsewhere. For as the *Independent* sneered: THINGS TURN SOUR FOR SUGAR. However, the *Guardian* flagged up that Sugar was responding to these sour times with admirable honesty. SUGAR OWNS UP, AND DOESN'T TRY TO SWEETEN THE PILL, wrote Roger Cowe. His article went on: 'Seldom are chairmen's statements of interest except to students of public relations. It is always interesting to see what depths can be represented as "a firm foundation for future growth" and what windfalls are credited to clear strategy and professional management. But company chairmen are not supposed to tell the truth – or certainly not the whole truth.

'All credit, then, to Amstrad founder and chairman Alan Sugar for owning up to a series of mistakes which have led to his company making the worst kind of history by reporting a drop in profits for the first time. Of course Mr Sugar is in a slightly more comfortable position than most company chairmen since he still owns nearly half the company. And he has always been one to speak his mind, usually at the expense of his City critics. But even so, his frankness is surprising as well as more than welcome and worthy of extensive quotation: "The result is below our expectations and our true potential due to a chain of events, some outside our control and others the results of our own mistakes."'

The frankness and sincerity continued unabashed. For he then opened his heart to the *Sunday Times* in a soul-searching and frank interview. 'Our problems are very simple,' Sugar said. 'We have had such phenomenal growth over the past few years that we are still operating with a management team you would expect to be running a company a fraction of our size. From an engineering point of view we had too small a team to take on too big a task and we are now paying the penalties in terms not only of our ability to design new products but to maintain our existing ranges.' He confessed that he had not kept a close enough eye on the company's financial situation. 'There is nobody to blame but ourselves. It was entirely our own naivety in thinking we could take on products as advanced as the new business personal computers so quickly. They represent a much bigger dimension in technology.'

Looking to his foreign subsidiaries, he said that their inventories had not been executed thoroughly enough. 'Previously, we didn't own the overseas distribution outlets. They were merely our customers, so we didn't have to worry about their inventories. When we took them over we severely underestimated the amount of head office support these people would need. We must strengthen ourselves in engineering and design,' he said, 'especially in our method of checking, testing and bringing products to the market so that they are rock solid as soon as they go into production. We've also got to get a team of heavy hitters on the financial side to improve our product planning and take much more firm control of inventories, especially in our overseas subsidiaries.'

The focus in the future for Amstrad would be clear, he said. It would involve 'continuing to design a stream of products and bringing them swiftly to market. We can't take two years to design products; it must continue to be other companies copying us two years later. I don't mean that we should hire a vast force of design people but we could do with more engineering foremen to manage the technical team.'

Other technology companies that had fallen into problems around this time chose to respond by going private again. Sugar said this was not an option he was considering for Amstrad for the time-being. 'I have personally made a lot of money out of the City,' he said. 'We chose to go into the public arena, and we enjoyed the benefits when we were a rising star. I'm not complaining now.' Again, this was a straightforward and clear-headed man addressing a tough time for his business in an honest and fearless way. Fortunately, he was about to receive a stroke of financial fortune that would help him get Amstrad back on its feet.

In September 1991, Amstrad sued American firm Seagate over some allegedly defective hard disc drives that had been supplied to Amstrad and subsequently damaged Amstrad's reputation. Seagate denied Amstrad's claims and promised to vigorously defend the action, which it said was entirely 'without merit'. It was to be a protracted and expensive legal battle. In May 1997 the case was finally settled in Amstrad's favour – and the company was awarded £57 million in damages – when Judge Humphrey Lloyd QC ruled that the disc drives had been faulty. Sugar was quick to put the case in context. 'Nobody will ever know where Amstrad would be today if this had not happened. The great efforts of myself and my small team were demolished. The financial award we have received today only goes some way to compensate us.'

The people of Seagate were stunned. 'I was shocked and appalled,' said their coincidentally named chief executive Alan Shugart. 'I think we got home-courted.' The *Guardian* noted the dramatic effect the result of this case would have on the fortunes of Amstrad. AMSTRAD HITS THE LEGAL JACKPOT cheered the headline. The story read: 'The fortunes of Amstrad, Alan Sugar's struggling electronics company, were transformed yesterday by a surprise court victory which will boost the company's value by nearly half. Amstrad won a decision in a case dating back to the late 1980s which will bring the once high-flying computer company a windfall of more than £100 million in damages and interest.'

True, the legal case had helped his company's financial fortunes, but Sugar's sincere and honest approach to his recent woes had helped too.

His philosophy in this regard is best summed up by the man himself. 'To keep yourself motivated when things go wrong, you need to analyse where things went wrong,' he says. Sounds simple, doesn't it? But there is a second layer to the analysis. 'You have to be very realistic. Don't try to blame the rest of the world. The blame only lies with you. Recognise that immediately.'

In a sense, Sugar's honesty is a welcome relic from a bygone era. There is a selflessness and integrity to it and to him. Not for him the self-reflection and self-help speak of the 21st century. Nor does he indulge in the tiresome 'me, me, me' obsession of so many nowadays. Not only is this old-fashioned in a very welcome way, there is also something British about it. Forget the pretentiousness of some of our Continental cousins, and set aside the self-help speak of the American people. Sugar is an old-fashioned Brit who largely eschews the complexities of modern business-speak.

For instance, when asked if there was a 'Sugar brand', he replied: 'Yes, Tate & Lyle.' Witty, and not without honesty. Indeed, if Sugar does have a brand then some would argue that honesty and wit are key components. 'We're interested in the mass-merchandising of anything,' he once said. 'If there was a market in mass-produced nuclear weapons, we'd market them too.' (There is a healthy arms trade in the world, but one takes his point.) Perhaps the real charm of Sugar's truthfulness is that it is unapologetic. How admirable that a man who has earned every penny of his considerable fortune should not feel the need to downplay or dismiss the fruits of his labour. His pride in his achievements is to be encouraged, although here, perhaps, he is being more American than British. The US is a country far more comfortable with success and the celebration of it than the UK.

Sugar is consistent in his relationship with straightforward communication. Some straight-talkers are shown to be astonishing hypocrites when they are on the receiving end of honesty from someone else, taking offence at just the sort of bluntness they would deliver themselves. However, Sugar has welcomed those who tell him it like it is. Some of his closest allies in the business world are far from shrinking violets. Witness the selection of businessmen and women he has chosen to conduct the interviews of *Apprentice* candidates in the penultimate round of the competition. The likes of property dealer Paul Kelmsley, trouble-shooter Claude Littner and Bordan Tkachuk, chief executive of Viglen Computers, can be accused of some things, but dishonesty is certainly not among them. All are unflinchingly to-the-point in dealing with the candidates, and then just as honest with Sugar in the subsequent boardroom briefing.

The bawdy banter between Sugar and the interview panel has become one of the delights of the series, as when Kelmsley jokingly winked at Sugar as he left the boardroom. 'Piss off!' was the boss's succinct reaction.

Not that everyone who watches the show so enjoys the interview round. Zena Everett, founder of recruitment firm Perriam And Everett, was critical of some of the responses. 'OK, we all know it's a TV reality show but comments such as "you're a contractor because no one is going to employ you" and "your CV is one of the most boring CVs I've ever read" hardly gives the right impression to any aspiring HR professionals watching,' she said.

All the same, Sugar clearly values their honesty. He is

naturally quite disappointed by those who do not show this prized quality. During his nine years in football during the 1990s, Sugar was disgusted by the lack of honesty he found among those who play the game. To him, football was far from being the beautiful game, as many often call it. Instead, he believed, it was an ugly affair, lacking the qualities he values most, and he remains dismissive of footballers as a breed to this day. 'They don't know what honesty or loyalty is,' he said.

To be fair, some players during his time at Tottenham Hotspur have been less than complimentary about him as well. Not that he believes we should spend a second of our time thinking about what footballers say about anything.

Asked by the *Daily Telegraph* in 2005 about an unspecified allegation dating back to the Spurs days, he stormed, 'Oh, do me a favour! Listen to a f***ing football player? Will you get real? I don't know why you're wasting your breath talking about what a f***ing footballer says. They're scum, total scum. They're bigger scum than journalists, don't you understand? They don't know what honest or loyalty is. They're the biggest scum that walk on this planet and, if they weren't football players, most of them would be in prison, it's as simple as that.'

Honest and straight to the point indeed. Strong language, too. As we have already seen, Sugar occasionally has turned the air (mildly) blue on *The Apprentice*. However, again there is a charm to his directness, seen in the fact he strongly believes there is a limit to how much bad language one should use on screen. He has criticised, for instance, TV chef Gordon Ramsay for his swear-word-ridden programmes. 'There are some minor expletives that I may use from time to time, but other than that I think it is unnecessary,' he said. There won't be any Ramsay-style cries of: 'Show me your f***ing balls' from Sugar anytime soon.

Although he angrily derides the lack of loyalty among footballers, Sugar is in no way naive about the world of business. He does not expect loyalty in this competitive sphere. 'When you wake up on a Monday morning, nobody anywhere in the world owes you a living,' he said in the 1980s. 'The minute someone offers a lower price or a better service, you will be dropped like a red hot brick. As long as you recognise that and don't expect any kind of loyalty or relationship, you can't go too far wrong.'

So, much as he has buckets of honesty and loyalty, and much as he values both assets where they exist, he is under no illusions as to how rare they are in business. It is a cut-throat world and one he is willing to compete in on its own terms.

As we have seen, Sugar has ensured that wherever possible he only employs those who welcome his style of speaking and operating. Consequently, his forthright style is accepted by those closest to him. For instance, Margaret Mountford, his *Apprentice* sidekick for the first five series of the show, took on the chin a cutting bon mot Sir Alan made about her. Distinguishing her from the salespeople of the world, he remarked that she would not be able to sell a book of matches.

'No, I've never seen myself as a little match girl,' she later agreed, adding that she is not a haggler either. 'Would I ever say, "If I buy three will you give me a discount?" No. It sticks in my throat. I won't buy anything in a market where you have to bargain. I really hate it.'

Just as she accepted his honesty, so too did he appreciate hers. 'I wasn't afraid to say my piece and he would listen,' she said of her time working with him in the show and before it. 'He knows I tell him what I think without worrying if he agrees or not. He doesn't like yes-men. And he doesn't like small talk. He won't ask about your holiday. He's a very shrewd, clever man and he judges people very carefully before he gives them a job.' Indeed, she speaks highly of his integrity in the face of his increasing wealth. 'Money can change people, but not Alan,' she insists. 'He still has his core values.'

As well as core values, he also has a manner about him that seems to somehow encourage others to reflect him: Sugar's ways are often infectious. Pip Greenwell was a graduate of Winchester public school and a senior partner in a City stockbroker firm. In 1979 he visited Sugar's then-shambolic office, squeezed between a train line and some derelict ground. As he entered the office, he had to manoeuvre round cardboard boxes and other debris. He held out his hand to the 32-year-old Sugar and offered his apologies for being late. 'I'm so terribly sorry we're late,' he began, but then added: 'but the f***ing traffic was awful.'

After a moment of uneasy silence – the language had surprised both parties – Sugar smiled and said: 'Thank God someone in the City speaks my sort of language.' It was a successful start to the meeting and set the tone for some useful discussions.

In internal Amstrad meetings Sugar very much valued straight talk. 'He rarely passes the time of day in his meetings,' wrote David Thomas in his superb work *Alan Sugar: The Amstrad Story*.

There was the same sort of directness when Sugar visited the factories that produced Amstrad products. During the 1970s he used the L&N plant in Kent. It was from here that musical equipment emerged – but not before Sugar had visited and had his own, characteristically delivered, say on matters. You can imagine the nerves twitching at the factory as the time of Sugar's arrival approached.

As Ron Nixon – the N of L&N – recalled: 'He was in bold all the time. He'd go round and rave and rant at anything that wasn't right.' Not that Nixon was a gentle soul himself. 'We used to have some real old slanging matches,' he said.

Closer to home, Sugar employed others who not only appreciated but almost mirrored his own remarkably direct way of speaking. One such man was Bob Watkins, a big, strong Essex man who cut a formidable figure.

Interestingly, his career had followed a not dissimilar path to Sugar's. He, too, had found himself frustrated in a Westminster job. Where Sugar had worked for the Department of Education and Science, Watkins had worked for the Ministry of Defence. He was just as unimpressed with the civil service crowd as Sugar had been.

'I couldn't believe what a bunch of wasters they were,' sneered Watkins. 'They didn't use their brains. Everything I was doing was being repeated and duplicated by other departments. Everything took longer than it should have.' Sounds like another man who spoke Sugar's language and Watkins was indeed soon pitching up at Amstrad's door having discovered, he says, that, 'Amstrad was at the rubbish end of the market, but I joined all the same.' Well, that's nothing if not to the point.

Once there, Watkins found that Sugar was often 'on his case'. He did not enjoy Sugar shadowing his moves – literally and metaphorically – watching over his shoulder. He wondered if Sugar was deliberately trying to unsettle him and told the boss that he'd had enough and was resigning. Sugar was keen to keep Watkins and, with the help of a pay rise, persuaded him to stay and give the place a second chance. Within months, though, he was once again feeling Sugar was on his back. Again, he threatened to walk. Again Sugar kept him with a pay rise. The boss was appreciative of Watkins's professional abilities, but also his honesty.

Watkins's succinct assessment of the 'wasters' at the

Ministry of Defence could easily have come straight from the mouth of Sugar, who was just as disdainful of the civil servant set and of corporate bureaucrats. 'There are those who are happy to be non-achievers in life,' he sneered, 'who get buried in a big corporation and flit from job to job. They will never change their ways and, in a way, you have to admire how they get away with it all their life, without doing a day's work.' They would never get away with it at Amstrad.

'There are others who are, I suppose, like me,' he said, 'who never expect anything for nothing and only know how to put one's head down and get on with the job. That is the type we at Amstrad attract.' (See the Hard Work and Enterprise chapter for evidence of just how fearsomely accurate this claim was.)

As Sugar moved into manufacturing computers, he was bang on the money and straight to the point in describing the Amstrad dream model. 'He looks at this thing, with its whacking great big keyboard and a monitor and he has visions of a girl at Gatwick airport where he checks himself in for his holidays. And he thinks, That's a real computer, not this pregnant calculator thing over there called a Sinclair.' This sort of talk cut through the brand-speak, the creation of which was beginning to become a business in itself. The brand consultants were soon to appear, delighted to charge you an arm and a leg in return for a catchy title to name your company. Would you have fancied your chances pitching up to Sugar and offering to 'brand' Amstrad for him? Your feet wouldn't have touched the ground.

When he read the first proofs of the instruction manual that would accompany an Amstrad computer, he was as succinct as ever. In a foretaste of the sort of summary he would offer to candidates' efforts in *The Apprentice* boardroom, he said: 'From an engineering point of view, the [manual] was fantastic. It had cross-references for every single detail of the Z80 processor. But that doesn't tell somebody how to write a quick letter about selling a lawn-mower.' Ever a man of the people, his efforts with the Amstrad computers might have sometimes confused the gentlemen geeks of the computer press, but they weren't his target.

'The pundits thought we were bloody mad again... They looked at us as the poor relation who needed to go to the mental asylum.' But, he boasted, he had the last laugh as he brought 'computing to the people who never even thought they would use a computer.'

More recently came his move into politics – hardly a profession celebrated in the public's perception for its honesty. However, his appointment as the Government's Enterprise Tsar surely confirmed for even the most doubting of cynics that here is an honest businessman. The House of Lords Appointments Commission conducts a thorough vetting of nominees. As well as security checks, they also examine media, government agency records and those of the Electoral Commission. For instance, they ask probing questions about 'the propriety of a nominee'. As the Commission itself explains, '[It] takes the view that in this context, propriety means first, the individual should be in good standing in the community in general and with particular regard to the public regulatory authorities, and second, the individual should be a credible nominee.'

As a Labour Party donor, Sugar's donations and relationship with the party were also scrutinised. 'The Commission believes that the best way of addressing this issue is to reach a view on whether or not the individual could have been a credible nominee if he or she had made no financial contribution,' it concludes. Again, the answer was 'yes' for Sugar.

Vindication came via different routes, as Sugar recalled. As we have seen, he had a lengthy correspondence with a doubter – and eventually won him over. 'A bloke here called Lord Oakeshott gave a few TV interviews saying that people like me shouldn't be allowed in the Lords because I supposedly run dodgy businesses and don't pay taxes in the UK – all rubbish, of course,' said Sugar. 'I've spent three months exchanging letters with him, until, in the end, he wrote me an apology. Now, I feel I've put him in his place. In fact,' he continued smilingly, 'I was thinking of photocopying it and putting it in all 600 cubby holes here as a message to others: don't you say anything about me unless I've actually done something wrong.'

As we shall see, another familiar figure in the corridors of Westminster was to regret questioning the appointment of Sugar. Even for a man as confident, courageous and wealthy as Sugar, to take on people in positions of political power is not something to be undertaken lightly. Did he not, an interviewer wondered, feel nervous going head-to-head with a political figure?

Sugar's answer displays the confidence he feels in his character and track record. 'No,' he fired back, 'because it was pretty clear to everyone except him that I hadn't done anything wrong. Most people have some skeletons in their cupboard, be it some girl they've had an affair with or someone they've treated unfairly, but nobody has ever been able to uncover a single one in mine because there are none: I'm a fair bloke. People make decisions about you when you're on TV, but in an institution like this they should be wise enough to know better.' He paused. 'And anyway, why shouldn't the Lords be for me?'

The clearance process was therefore a great vindication – if one were needed – for Sugar in the court of public opinion. However, would Sugar's political appointment mean he would have to temper his honest, clear-eyed assessments of the world? Would, in short, the tough-talker sell out, as so many people who enter the political sphere do? Political interests and ambition have clouded the clear thinking of many a man and woman. Would Sugar go down that path? The answer came within weeks of his appointment, when he pointedly criticised the Government's role on employment training places for young people in Britain. The star of *The Apprentice* was not, it seemed, impressed with Brown's record on apprenticeships.

'This country has had a proud history of apprenticeships, but they have been scandalously neglected in recent times,' he said. 'We have seen some progress recently. I was pleased to hear the numbers of apprentices have trebled to around 225,000 during the past ten years. It is clear that we have got a way to go, however, if an apprenticeship is to be a viable option for everyone – younger and older – who wants to do one.'

He had a point. Youth unemployment was nearing the million mark. 'The Government needs to show its commitment,' he said. Noting news that further investment was planned, he added: 'That investment needs to be maintained if apprenticeships are to be a long-term success. I believe that, if there is enough demand from employers, school leavers and adults wanting to try an apprenticeship, then the money will follow.' So there you have it – as honest and genuine as ever.

Sugar might have been given a way into politics by Gordon Brown, and he might have huge respect for the Labour politician, but there was no way he was about to 'sell out' and fail to speak out when he thought it was needed. Surely, one must believe, Brown would not have expected anything different, not least since – as we saw at the opening of this chapter – he is fully aware of Sugar's blunt ways. Brown's premiership has been in many ways a rather unremarkable and disappointing one. However, kudos must surely be given to the man for taking on someone as outspoken as Sugar. A yes-man Sugar is not, and one wonders how many previous leaders would have been assured enough to bring him into the fold.

Brown might have appreciated Sugar's tough-talking, even if some of it has made Government uncomfortable. Fans of *The Apprentice* certainly enjoy his outspoken nature, too. But of course not all recipients and witnesses of Sugar's honesty have been quite so pleased with the experience. Comedian Alan Carr received a lashing from Sugar during the 2009 instalment of *Comic Relief Does The Apprentice*. He found Sugar's abrasiveness difficult to deal with. 'Just how scary is he? He's horrible. I thought because we were celebrities he'd tone it down, but he was vile and laid into me. I used to take the mickey out of the contestants when they cried on *The Apprentice*, but he had me in tears. I was gulping and had a lump in my throat!'

Another comedian to turn the honesty table on Sugar is David Mitchell, who defended Sugar's appointment as Enterprise Tsar – but for sarcastic reasons. 'Sir Alan Sugar is perfectly suited to the job of "Enterprise Tsar" because it's not a job – it's an exercise in presentation, just like his role on the BBC,' he said. Mitchell then derided the Conservative Party for lambasting the appointment. 'In less bewildered times, an ambitious opposition would welcome the opportunity to ridicule such a disastrously craven Government appointment. Instead, they're meanly trying to block it because they're annoyed they didn't think of it themselves.' You can't win them all, Lord Sugar.

Ironically, it was only as he entered politics that Lord Sugar was asked to produce his first ever CV. Writing of what he had learned to date, he penned: 'Obtained greater understanding of the lack in honesty and integrity of those I met and dealt with.'

In the final analysis, his honesty comes as a result of a very simple complementary quality he possesses in abundance: self-confidence. 'I don't give a monkey's what anyone else thinks,' he said. Expanding on this stance later, he got even closer to the point and dismissed the feelings of those who dislike his style of speech. 'Sometimes people don't like what I say, the way I express it, for example,' he said. 'I use an expression that people use sometimes, that you don't like hearing the home truth sometimes, and I'm ... I think that what the Government needs is a refreshing person like me who tells it as it is. And you'll get newspapers like the *Daily Mail* who love it. I mean, I'm cannon fodder for them. I am their bread and butter, particularly when they deliberately take my words out of context.'

He is under no doubt that many in the media dislike him. When he is interviewed, particularly by newspaper journalists, he is hilariously to the point at times. He was asked by Lynne Barber of the *Observer* what it *meant* to say that he owned £150 million. 'Well… cash. You know what cash is, don't you?' he mocked.

Barber replied that, yes, she knew what cash was but found it hard to picture such a large amount. Did he keep it under his mattress, she wondered jokingly?

He gave her a blank stare and replied, 'Well, obviously it's in the bank. With all due respect, you are very, very naive.'

Later in the interview he erupted twice at Barber, first when she attempted to include his wife in the discussion, and then when she asked Sugar whether all his friends were wealthy people. 'Do you know, you're starting to annoy me. Really, you are. And I'd advise you to tone it down. I am a businessman and I've been successful and what you get from that is wealth, OK? But it's not the be all and end all. Money is not my god. So let's bung that idea out once and for all, shall we?'

Honesty is always the best policy, they say. Certainly, even when it is tough to deliver the truth, it must be the kindest way to deal with any other person. However, one should not get at all carried away with the idea that honesty and harshness always go hand in hand. Frequently, Sugar shows how even in the delivery of truth he can be kind and gentle.

Television journalist Daisy McAndrew spent several months with a group of unemployed college leavers. She took two who had particularly low confidence levels to meet Lord Sugar. Lucas and Matt were nervous before meeting Sugar, but he was kindness personified with them. Noting their nerves and the way that their situation had shattered their confidence, he said that he once felt the same. 'I had no confidence at all but all it takes is for you to get out of your comfort zone in front of someone important, who doesn't then think you're a total muppet, and your confidence will grow.'

McAndrew was impressed. 'They went into his office scared stiff and pretty much mute,' she remembered. 'They came out beaming. Alan Sugar – Lord Sugar to us – may well be fantastically rude to journalists like me, but that's just fine, because he proved he does care about the struggle facing a million unemployed youngsters like Matt and Lucas. And they certainly need someone like him fighting their corner.'

They certainly do. However, a truthful nature is not enough to take a man to the riches he has earned and to a lofty position in government. Plenty more good values are needed too. Chief among them is hard work.

CHAPTER TWO

HARD WORK AND ENTERPRISE

It was in the streets of East London, in the early hours of the morning, that Sugar first showed his work ethic. As a child he earned his first wages by wandering around the estate, knocking on people's doors and asking if they had any fizzy drink bottles he could redeem at the local shop. A small fee was available to anyone who returned the bottles to the shop and he was amazed that everyone was not automatically taking them back to claim their deposit.

'I'd take 12 bottles back to the sweet shop downstairs and get a shilling for them,' recalled Sugar. 'I used to think to myself, These people must be mad. All I had to do was walk downstairs with the bottles.'

It was the first sign of the Sugar way of working. Here were so many of the methodologies which drive him to this day: eyeing an opportunity, keeping it simple, enterprise, effort and exasperation at the perceived lethargy of others.

Mostly, though, he was just enjoying making the money, even if it was just a shilling a go. Could a similar task be set for candidates on *The Apprentice*? Sugar would truly be able to 'walk it as he talks it' in setting one, and watching the assembled candidates forced to perform such a simple yet unglamorous operation would presumably separate the wheat from the chaff with stark clarity.

One can easily imagine, though, the excitement of Sugar as he gathered the bottles and proudly took them to the local shop for his reward. As he walked home, shilling in pocket, he would have shaken his head in surprise that it was him making the money out of other people's bottles. This was a valuable lesson for him to learn – that the world was full of opportunities that other people were either not aware of or not of a mind to pursue. All he had to do was identify the opening and pursue it vigorously. He had little problem with either of these challenges and as such was already showing the sort of entrepreneurial qualities that would see him rise all the way to the *Sunday Times* Rich List later in life.

Soon he would notice the division between those who picked up on the chances life throws up and those who do not, even as he despaired of the way his father went about his professional life and vowed never to follow the same path. In the meantime, however, it felt good, that shilling, sitting in his pocket as he made his way home. And all he had needed to do to acquire it was return a few bottles to a store.

He had got the taste of pocketing cash and it was through a not unrelated, if more ambitious, route that he arrived at his next money-making scheme. At 13 years of age he was given a present that would refresh more than his thirst. In those days, a ginger beer plant was popular in many British households. Thought to have originated from the Royal Botanical Gardens in Kew, this was not a plant in the sense of a green stem with leaves or flowers. Instead, the ginger beer plant was a sloppy white mass, comprising bacteria, yeast and fungus. This would be kept in a jar by excited Brits and topped up daily with teaspoons of ginger and sugar, together with lemon juice and water. The substance would then produce a bubbly liquid to be siphoned out of the jar and put into bottles.

Sugar soon had his own ginger beer to sell and was ready to take on the soft drink giants of the world – or at least in his immediate surroundings. He would sell his home-brewed (or home-fermented, to be precise) ginger beer to his fellow kids on the estate. Undercutting the likes of Coca-Cola, he proved a popular merchant and was soon bringing in a semi-decent income. His entrepreneurial streak was increasing as he sought more and more ways to pocket cash. More famously, he also worked with a local greengrocer. He would rise in the early hours of Saturday morning to boil beetroot for the man, again earning himself some much-welcomed spending money.

'It wasn't a case of deciding to do that,' he says of this unglamorous Saturday job. 'It was quite common for people who lived in my council block to have a Saturday job, a holiday job, a paper round or whatever. It was necessary – if you wanted your own pocket money you had to go and get it yourself.' He took whatever jobs were on offer. When one opportunity disappeared or was outshone by something better, he simply moved on. Some were more exciting than others, but whatever the challenge and opportunity was, he was happy to take it and to approach it with his sense of focus, determination and effort.

Another job he took was with a friend of the Sugar family. The friend ran a market stall in London and Sugar would traipse along to help out as the stall holder sold various materials, including linen. Sugar enjoyed the hustle and bustle of the market atmosphere. As ever, his entrepreneurial streak shone through and he decided that he did not need the apron-strings of a family friend. He could make it in this world on his own. Well, not entirely on his own but without the supervision of an adult. Instead, he gathered up a gang of mates and they opened their own stall, selling cleaning liquids. Their youthful voices could be heard proudly hawking their goods to the passers-by. It felt good to be out there, seizing the moment and, on a good day, making some money. He has regularly sent *Apprentice* candidates to markets, often as an early task in each series. For instance, in one series he sent them to sell fish on London market stalls. There is a democratic side to this way of selling and the market, more than many arenas, quickly reveals who is a good, dedicated salesman and who is not. These tasks have always been incredibly entertaining and usefully revealing for Sugar. Again, he can walk it as he talks it when he sends candidates to sell on the streets.

He was out there selling as a youngster, first with a family friend and then with his mates. They were becoming involved in the fine tradition of street trading that features so proudly in the history of east London. From New Spitalfields market in Leyton, to the Billingsgate market in Poplar, Shoreditch's Brick Lane and Ridley Road in Dalston, the streets of east London have long resonated with the cries of the street trader.

Next came work that some would perhaps find more surprising for Sugar to be involved in. He acquired a cheap camera and turned from Alan Sugar, market trader, to Alan Sugar, photographer. The latter title was the precise wording he put on the back of the photographs he took of neighbours and friends of the Sugar family. He had taken the odd snap already, as more of a boyish hobby than a career. Then one day he decided to turn it into a financial enterprise.

'People want pictures of their kids, always,' he recalled, 'and grandparents want pictures of their grandkids more than anything else. So I went straight to the grandparents and said to them, "I'll photograph your children for half-a-crown." And the answer was always, "Yes, yes, yes, yes." They could never have enough pictures of their grandchildren.' He later admitted that the photographs were nothing to keep professional photographers awake at night, but once more he had spotted an opportunity, chased it and found that he could make a success of it. He would develop the photographs in his own bedroom, keeping costs down.

Soon it was time for Sugar to go the more conventional route of taking on Saturday morning jobs, as many an adolescent boy does to this day. These included one at a department store in east London. The management of the store were so impressed with the salesmanship that Sugar showed during his Saturday shift that they asked him if he would like to take on a full-time job there and then. 'I seriously believe I've got an inborn talent,' he said later of his selling ability. 'I've got an inbuilt aptitude for trading and dealing and scenting the way the wind is blowing.'

This blend of selling genius and a keen eye for an opportunity reaped him monetary awards. He would save most of his proceeds, rather than spending it or flashing it around as some of his contemporaries did. 'I was quite a good saver as a kid,' he says. 'It was always indoctrinated into me from my family that you had to save your money.'

His family were hard workers, just like Sugar himself, but they lacked his fiercely independent streak. For them, one worked hard for others, not for one's own business. One of his uncles ran a shop selling hardware goods, but beyond that there was no immediate equivalent to Sugar in the family tree. That said, his Uncle John was an imaginative man. A press article was written about how he would liven up his shop by putting stickers with witty captions onto his stock. It's the sort of gimmick that brightens up a shop, gets it noticed and increases its profits. Like an old-fashioned version of the sort of trick that would win the approval of Sugar in the boardroom after an *Apprentice* task had been completed. Other than that, though, the family lacked entrepreneurial figures for Sugar to look up to.

'We were very working-class people,' his sister Daphne told author David Thomas. All the same, the environment motivated him. But how?

Sugar has looked back at the circumstances he grew up in to explain how they spurred him on to better himself and his parents. 'I suppose you would call it poverty now,' says Sir Alan, 'but that's just the way it was. But from a very young age I knew I wanted more than that. My objective was to make some money – make more money than my dad. That was all I ever set out to do. I didn't want to rely on anyone else. I didn't want a boss. I wanted independence. I wanted to control my own destiny.'

During his earliest years, Sugar was blissfully unaware of how unsteady and insecure his father's income was. Nathan Sugar worked in the garment trade. He was the last human hand on the garments before the machines sewed the items together. It was a reasonably well-paying job, but one that had little security. In the post-war years this was particularly true and Nathan was often unable to find work for weeks at a time. Once Sugar reached his teenage years he began to realise just what a worry this was for his parents. 'They simply told him on Monday morning, "Sorry, there's no work, don't come in." And he used to take it very badly.'

Sugar was determined to not follow this fate. To be clear, Sugar never felt his father lacked in effort. He was admiring of how hard his father worked. 'He did a very good job of bringing up a family of four children in very tough times,' he said. Nathan did indeed try to adapt to the insecurity of his profession by trying new ways to increase his chances of regular income. He knocked on the doors of new factories and introduced himself, hoping for more options. He sat up at night, making children's coats at home. He then sold the coats to the mothers of the area, who would snap up the homemade coats for special occasions, such as the Jewish celebration of Bar Mitzvah. Ever on the lookout for an opportunity to get an advantage in his trade, he started taking evening classes in garment work. These were all fine ways to seek an advantage in the garment trade, and tactics Sugar would grow to appreciate. Neighbours of the family, too, recall Nathan as a hard-working man.

So it was not a lack of effort that Sugar perceived in his father, rather a lack of entrepreneurism and risk-taking spirit. 'He had people rushing after him to make coats for them,' he recalls of his father, 'but the more people he had rushing after him, the more he got nervous. He could have opened his own shop. He could have made coats. He was a very intelligent man. The problem was he would not take a risk.' Instead, Sugar recalls, his father was a 'very big worrier'. Indeed, the same neighbours who noted his willingness to work also recall Nathan as a man who was old ahead of his time. Perhaps it was the worry, the stress weighing on his mind, that occasionally turned Nathan into an angry man.

It was against this backdrop that Sugar made the most of his schooling, where he learned some interesting skills. He attended Joseph Priestley, a secondary technical school in east London. It was based in a decaying building but Sugar speaks fondly of his time there. 'I could still to this day build a brick wall if I had to,' he once said, 'and I can still recite parts of Shakespeare. I can turn a lathe and read or draw a technical drawing. It was an amazing school.'

He enjoyed studying science and engineering and also took great pleasure from classes in metalwork and technical drawing. Those who taught him back then later expressed surprise that he had made such a success of his life, as they found him in no way extraordinary during his childhood. All the same, his ambition and vision was always on the rise.

So what was schoolboy Sugar like? He remembers that he was 'not a ruffian' but admits that there was 'always plenty of talk' at the Brookehouse School in Upper Clapton, Hackney, which Joseph Priestley became following a merger with Mount Pleasant, a secondary modern. A school report sent to his parents recorded that the adolescent Sugar was 'an able boy' but 'must take more care in the presentation of his work. A great improvement in his ability, but it is often misapplied. Alan is broadening his sphere of activities.'

More interesting and revealing was the passage that covers Sugar's involvement in the sporting side of the curriculum. The teacher was full of praise for his pupil who turned in 'a good year's work', adding, 'Alan has represented the house in football and rugby. He has helped in the organisation of the teams. Well done Alan.' Sugar would later take control of a football club, though not on the field, of course.

The schoolboy Sugar was a dab hand at maths, too. He puts this down to one teacher in particular, who he can still recall. 'I remember Mr Grant, the maths master, because even though he gave up on me, I managed to pass my O-level,' says the generous Sugar. 'He was a real eccentric. We used to call him Theta Grant because he made us laugh when he wrote the Greek letter theta on the blackboard. He was accident-prone. He'd come into school with his face smashed in or a broken arm. There were all sorts of rumours going round, but we never found out the cause of his injuries. When I discovered that the maths O-level syllabus involved something called calculus, which was supposed to be really difficult, I was fascinated. I've always enjoyed a challenge. I'm a quick learner and have a photographic memory. Within three or four weeks, I became the whiz-kid of calculus, which got me through the exam. Grant couldn't believe it.'

Seeing this reaction made Sugar determined to work hard and go his own way in business. Yet it was this same schooling that led to him taking his initial wrong turn in life. As we have seen, he took his first job in the Civil Service. Poor Sugar was driven to boredom and despair as he worked in the dreary environment of the statistics department of the Ministry of Education and Science. He had taken this unlikely role as a result of the subjects that he enjoyed at school.

'Science – this was something I had always been interested in,' he remembered. 'Statistics, maths – I wasn't too bad at that. So I thought I'd go for it.' So bored was he by the harsh reality that he clock-watched all day and could not wait to get home. This was not because of a lack of work ethic, merely of sheer frustration at the stiff and stuffy environment he found himself in. Indeed, so keen was he to work in general that he was probably the only person working in his building who also had a Saturday job elsewhere, at a clothes shop in the West End of London, followed by another at an East End chemist. He remains a hard worker to this day.

That Sugar is an enterprising man might seem an obvious statement to make. However, he is fundamentally so. 'The UK is poised for more enterprise,' he said in the 1980s. 'Not everyone can be an entrepreneur, but people have a fixation that Shell or BP are the backbone of the country. They're not. The actual backbone of the country is "Fred" with six employees in the garden centre, or in the garage. They're the ones who employ the majority of people in this country. Being employed in the old-fashioned way isn't that available any more. People have got to start thinking about doing things for themselves.'

Here, perhaps, he was speaking not just to the nation but also sending a message to his father. Nobody can doubt that Nathan worked hard and was a great father. However, for Sugar there was no following in his father's footsteps professionally: he was by nature too enterprising to do that.

One of his earliest initiatives came when he was selling record turntables through Amstrad. The plastic covers that prevented the turntable from getting dusty were a vital part of the early hi-fi – and an expensive part at that. The use of acrylic – and lots of it – made them costly to produce. Sugar would not take any part of the process as gospel and decided to investigate if there was a lower-cost alternative. So he picked up the phone and called a long list of organisations who worked in the field of plastic manufacturing.

'I decided to find out how they were made,' he remembered. 'I'm a quick learner, when I want to be.' He was soon learning about a new method. 'I found out about injection moulding, how it was done, and got someone to make me a few thousand.' That someone was, he said, 'the cheapest bloke going' and he caused Sugar a few headaches. The project was supposed to be completed in three months but ended up taking five. 'There was heartache and aggravation there,' Sugar said.

However, finally the tool was complete and he was able to make the covers more cheaply than anyone else. 'Until then, I'd been buying stuff at £1 each and hustling to sell it at £1.10. With the plastic tops, I became a producer, making something at four shillings which I sold for a quid. I'd risen above being just a buyer and seller.'

The injection-moulding machine cost Sugar £1,805, and he was soon reaping the rewards, selling them to the hi-fi stores of Tottenham Court Road (a street in London's West End dominated by such outlets) at a huge mark-up. They were then selling them to their customers at another mark-up and everybody was laughing all the way to the bank. None were laughing louder than Sugar, though. He was not only turning in a tidy project as thousand-strong orders flew in for the covers, he was also taking his business in a whole new direction.

'We came out of the era where I was just distributing all those wholesale imports into an era of becoming a manufacturer,' he remembered.

He was a business magician in those early days, always finding a way to get customers into shops and parted from their cash in return for his goods. One such magic trick was to lure customers into stores by advertising low-price or 'lead-in' products and then make sure that next to the cheap product was a superior and more expensive version.

'The salesman Dixonises them,' he explained, referring to the one-time leading electrical products store on Britain. 'He jumps on them and says, "Well, that one is the all-singing, all-dancing, more powerful, double-cassette, blah-de-blah." Nine times out of ten the customer will pay it off on credit, which works out at £1 a month more for the better one. The truth is we advertise the target lead-in price products, knowing that they will often end up being the lower sales.'

Sugar was ever a man who worked not just hard, but sensibly. As one retail contact recalled, if you went to Sugar with a difficult request he might initially be unsure of whether the request would be fulfilled. But a few days later he would phone with the solution: 'You know that thing we were talking about? Well, I've been thinking about it and this is what I've come up with…' No wonder the contact viewed Sugar as 'a guy who would work on how it could be done, rather than on why it couldn't'.

In the late 1980s, his entrepreneurial spirit began to be widely recognised in the business world and reflected in the media. In 1987, *Fortune* magazine named him one of Europe's 'new entrepreneurs' and lavished praise on him. 'Sugar, who grew up in a working-class neighbourhood in London's East End and began his business career selling car radio antennas from the back of a rented van, owns Amstrad stock worth more than $650 million. The value of his shares is 45 times what it was six years ago.' It added: 'The Old World's new entrepreneurs are more marketing-oriented than their predecessors.'

Sugar was quoted as saying: 'We produce products that people want, not some boffin's ego trip.'

The article captured the climate of the 1980s in Europe and said that Britain led the way in this new enterprising spirit. 'Conservative Prime Minister Margaret Thatcher has been womanfully striving to instil what she calls "an enterprise culture". By cutting Britain's top income tax rate from 98 per cent to 60 per cent, liberalising the treatment of stock options and granting hefty tax credits to individuals investing in start-ups, Thatcher has transformed her country's once declining small-business sector into a prodigious job creator. Since 1982 British business – mostly small new companies – has produced all but 200,000 of the 1.1 million new jobs created in Europe.'

It was shaping up as a decade of enterprise in the UK and Sugar was being heralded widely as a key figure in this mood. In the same year, he was described by *The Times* as 'Cockney-born Mr Sugar', one of the men 'who hold the aces' in business-driven times. His fame was proving international and cross-continental. The *New York Times* called Sugar 'Europe's most successful entrepreneur of the 1980s' in 1987.

There were three more years of the decade but, for the *New York Times*, 'the blunt, burly and bearded Mr Sugar' had already out-classed the rest. Looking to the future, the piece concluded that 'most agree it is hard to predict what consumer products will attract Mr Sugar's aggressive marketing talents.'

He was also to receive praise for his enterprising ways from none other than Rupert Murdoch. After Sugar provided the satellite dishes for the launch of Sky, Murdoch was full of praise for the enterprising and hard-working spirit he found in his colleague. 'He's very entrepreneurial, a tremendous worker. In negotiations, he's a master of detail. I found he came to the point, to the bottom line very quickly. He's been very straight with me – totally. He's kept his word on everything.' Might they work together again? 'I'd be surprised if there aren't other things we do with him.'

Sugar also crossed paths professionally with other business giants of that era, including Clive Sinclair. It was an unlikely partnership as the pair were different in so many ways. Sinclair is a gentle and rather posh man, whereas Sugar is tough-talking and working class. This did not trouble Sinclair, however. 'I found Alan Sugar a delightful man to deal with,' he said. 'He tended to say, "This is the deal." He never tried to improve his position or deviate from what he said he would do. He was very straightforward and clear-headed. He was very pleasant company, enjoyable to meet – a witty man.'

Not all of Sinclair's staff were quite so positive, according to Sugar. He felt they thought they were dealing with 'a boy who had just got Bar Mitzvahed...

someone with too much money and didn't know what I was doing.' He did know what he was doing, though, and thanks to his hard-working approach to the deal, Amstrad took over Sinclair's computer operations. The deal made waves around the world. SINCLAIR RESEARCH SOLD ran the headline in the *New York Times*. The *International Herald Tribune* called the deal the 'most widely followed $7million corporate transaction in British history'.

'Sinclair forced to sell patents to pay debts,' said *The Times*. Sugar had benefited from another situation by pouncing fast. Once more he had kept his eye on the ball and reaped the rewards.

Not that Lord Sugar is so focused and hard working to the detriment of his personal life. From the earliest years of Amstrad, he has always endeavoured to keep standard business hours. He believes that if time is managed sensibly then the standard 9am-5pm should be enough to get everything done in the day. Not for him the stereotyped existence of the business giant who only makes such a success of his career by working night and day, taking few holidays and allowing them to be constantly interrupted by telephone calls. Sugar believes that enormous success can go hand in hand with a sensible work/life balance. As a family man he would find it hard to operate any other way, although at times he did allow work to cast a shadow over his home life.

'Once he started in business, that was [also] his hobby,' his sister Daphne recalled. He once spent most of a family holiday in Majorca mulling over how to break through into the Comet chain. In the main, however, he kept an admirable balance between work and home.

When the company was based in Tottenham, north London, its hours of work were very strict. The office opened at 9am on the dot and closed its doors at 5.15pm. You could almost set your watch by this. Sugar's love of conventional hours was aided by the fact that – come what may – the security team for the building would lock the door at 5.15pm every day. Indeed, back in those early days it was far from unheard of in the final minutes leading to that deadline to witness employees desperately gathering their belongings and making a bolt for the exit. They had to: if they were not out of the office by 5.15pm they would be locked in for the night. Now that's a good way to focus your staff on good timekeeping. One client that Amstrad worked with recalls that if he was on the telephone to a contact there in the afternoon, he could sense their anxiety that they didn't end up locked into the office overnight. 'They tended to be very nervous in the last ten minutes,' he recalled.

Never has Sugar felt the need to pretend he works any harder than he does. 'I take my holidays,' he said in 1980 during an interview to tie in with Amstrad's flotation, 'and I think five days' work is enough. If a job isn't finished on Friday, it can wait until Monday.'

So what did, in those heady days, a working day between Monday and Friday look like for Sugar? He would stay at his desk whenever possible, keeping any trips or meetings with outside people to a minimum. He would often miss lunch entirely or simply have a quick sandwich at his desk. He expected hard work from his employees, it was true. However, what he certainly did not want were empty gestures of effort. Working late in the office to try and impress the boss would have been a mostly futile gesture at Amstrad in the 1980s. Instead, the only way forward was to work hard and effectively during the working hours. The late bolt for the door continued after Amstrad moved from north London. 'Even today,' one employee said in the 1980s, 'if you stand in front of the exit at a minute to five, you get trodden into the carpet.'

When Amstrad moved to Brentwood, Essex, the streamlined, hardworking ethic barely changed. Focused isn't the word: a visitor to the office compared the operation to one manned by a team of 'Israeli paratroopers'. Another who arrived to take up a new job during the Brentwood era said of his first impressions of his boss and new colleagues: 'I seemed to be working with a bunch of football hooligans who were trading.'

It was a small team of men and women much like Sugar himself: full of common sense, drive and aggression. He had managed to shape the team in his own image and could look over them proudly, sitting in

the middle of his ninth floor, open plan office. He had a
well-worn leather armchair to sit on, and again the
message was clear: this is a lean, mean, fighting machine
more than it is a corporate jolly. Surrounding his desk
were a collection of smaller desks on which were
chaotically placed some Amstrad computers. One can
almost imagine Sugar paraphrasing the announcement at
the beginning of the American music drama *Fame*:
'Success costs, and right here in Brentwood is where you
start paying – with sweat.' He would have cut an
impressive but not-to-be-messed-with figure. He was the
boss and there would be no mistaking that.

He expected all his staff to be accessible, however lofty
their position. Ken Ashcroft was an Amstrad finance
director at this time. When auditors visited the company
they were taken aback at how accessible Ashcroft was.
When they had queries that needed addressing they
would, at most companies, need to go through a
frustrating, laborious process as the matter was passed
slowly up the chain of command to a distant director,
who they might never meet directly. Not at Amstrad.
There they had direct and immediate access to Ashcroft.
They were impressed and very surprised. One of the
auditors actually suggested to Ashcroft that he might be
a bit too accessible. 'With my chairman,' he replied, 'if I
closed my door, he would tear it off its hinges.'

The Amstrad culture was essentially non-negotiable.
Anyone who turned up to work at the company had to

fit in quickly, whether they felt like they were surrounded by football hooligans or not. As marketing executive Malcolm Miller told David Thomas: 'We've taken young, bright graduates. But more importantly they have to have the right culture. They have to be entrepreneurial and enterprising. They have to be able to rewrite the rule book, if necessary.'

Miller also expanded on the hard-working atmosphere at Amstrad and what Sugar required of those who worked there. 'If you haven't got a sense of urgency... and you just want to be a bureaucrat pushing people and paper around, it doesn't work here. We will not become like the people who sit on committees all day long pushing papers around, theorising about some activity that might increase the brand share by 0.1 per cent to raise at next month's marketing committee. That's not us.'

Crucially, meetings were kept short and Miller explains that if an important phone call were to come during a meeting, it would not be acceptable at Amstrad to fob the caller off with the immortal 'He's in a meeting' line. No, the employee would leave the meeting and take the call.

Anyone taking a trip around the office in the mid-1980s would have been under no illusion as to the lack of 'corporate bullshit', as Sugar might have put it. In the meeting room the foam was spilling out of the chairs, and the walls of the office were mostly plain white, interrupted only by dirty charts with roughly-written statistics on them. Take a step into the boardroom and you would have encountered another shambolic scene: Amstrad stock was piled up against the walls. It was a world away from the swish, minimalist decor of the boardroom of *The Apprentice*. Sugar wanted to put his efforts into making the company work, not making the office tidy and ordered. Anyone stopping by to offer advice on *feng shui* would have been given an abrupt response by the boss. He was on a mission and no more enamoured by far-Eastern philosophies than continental air-kissing or American self-help speak. Good old hard work? He was up for a bit of that. 'He has an incredibly focused mind,' wrote one who knew him then.

There were plentiful rewards and benefits to employees from this culture. As Miller explained, from the moment someone joined Amstrad, they would have opportunities rarely enjoyed elsewhere. 'We allow them to make important decisions, which they couldn't do in a larger company,' he said. 'We allow them to feel part of the problems and opportunities, successes and failures we have every day.' This set up a sink-or-swim process. 'Certain people like responsibility,' he continued. 'They like to feel they can change the face of one of Amstrad's projects – they can do a deal with a big software company on a promotion, they can come up with a new creative idea for an advert, they can find a new retailing opportunity that makes a big difference.' This was refreshing for the new staff, as was the approachability and visibility of the boss.

Miller would sometimes organise opportunities for staff to meet quickly with the boss and pitch ideas to him. This was a far cry from huge corporate firms where the top man would be a mysterious figure, to be occasionally glanced photographically in the pages of the in-house newsletter. It was far from rare for new Amstrad members to be sitting across the table from the boss, discussing their ideas. 'They always find it very stimulating,' said Miller. 'I say to them, "Let's show Alan this idea of yours." He'll sit and deliberate and they'll get a chance to argue. Some of them will argue, but if we don't like the idea we say so immediately.'

Even away from his desk, Lord Sugar is a hard grafter. In 2007, concerned about his weight and health, he took up cycling. It had a dramatic effect on his appearance, turning the once ageing and bloated Sugar into a lean and youthful looking man, despite competition in his early attempts as he came across more experienced cyclists.

'They would say, "Passing by left. Have a nice day." I thought, Sod all that "have a nice day" stuff. I wanted a faster bike. So a shop in Boca Raton measured me up for the latest Pinarello, no doubt trying to flog me a bike that offered them the best retail margin.' How satisfying it was to give these new wheels a spin. Soon, he was overtaking others. 'With my new bike I was now saying "Passing by left" to other riders and I would do the 40 miles in half the time, soon increasing to 60.'

Still, one should not get carried away at Sugar's age

and he quickly learned to get things in perspective. 'When I begin thinking I am the new Lance Armstrong I get a wake-up call. Young lads and girls still pass me by at 28-30 miles an hour but I can give them a run sometimes for a five-mile stretch.' He denies that he shaved his legs as pro cyclists such as Armstrong do. 'I don't bloody shave my legs,' he says firmly. 'I am just not that hirsute, except on my face.'

He has encountered the odd scrape, as many long-distance cyclists have. 'I have come back a bit cut up at times, but I usually keep quiet about it as Ann will fret,' he said referring to his wife. 'But thank God I have had no breakages.

'I like riding alone. It is a good time to chew over problems, discuss them with myself and sort them out,' he says. 'I have my BlackBerry whirring away in my pocket and usually I stop after a while and answer emails.' He can do 50 miles in under three hours, which is impressive for a man of any age. Many fit men much younger would struggle to beat him.

This love of two-wheeled travelling is nothing new, incidentally. 'I used to do up bikes and we would sell a few, too,' he remembers. 'It was just a kids' thing really, but I got pretty handy with fixing bikes. I remember I had to have one with chrome forks, which was the thing back then.'

Cycling is not the only activity that sees his work hard/play hard equation work. He took it up to replace another of his hobbies – tennis. After prolonged groin problems and several operations, however, he was forced to scale down his tennis, playing only on soft surfaces for short periods of time. 'Otherwise the impact begins to hurt,' he said.

Prior to these problems he had been a keen tennis player since the 1980s, even arranging a star-studded tennis event at the Royal Albert Hall in June 1989. The evenings were light and warm as summer dawned and the Wimbledon tennis fortnight was just around the corner. Among the television personalities to compete in the Amstrad-sponsored event were *Minder* actor Dennis Waterman, comic Jimmy Tarbuck and chat-show legend Terry Wogan. Footballer Bobby Moore was present too.

However, the star of the show in terms of organising and competing was Sugar himself. He stormed to the semi-finals, where it was very much a battle of the business giants. Sugar was drawn against Virgin tycoon Richard Branson. Both men had a partner and the doubles match was fiercely contested amid a boisterous atmosphere. 'Come on, Alan!' chanted many in the audience as Sugar and his partner beat team Branson and sailed into the final, which they also won. However, the real winner was the Muscular Dystrophy Group, for which the evening raised a wonderful £170,000. As we shall see in the Charity and Inspiration chapter, Sugar is a man who loves to give to good causes. All the same, the competitive tycoon was delighted to have won. All that work and effort he had put into perfecting his technique, practising while on holiday in the Catskill Mountains and in Florida, and at home at weekends, had paid off.

Perhaps – and one can only speculate on this – part of Sugar's frustration with footballers during his time at Tottenham Hotspur was born out of a belief that sportsmen often have it easy. True, any professional sportsman will have made many sacrifices on his way to the top of the game. And though Tottenham Hotspur were no FC Barcelona in the 1990s, it was still a mid-table club in England's top division. When he heard of footballers demanding new wage increases and bonuses and learned of them negotiating via aggressive agents for lucrative commercial and endorsement deals, might Sugar have felt that some of them were in it for the money rather than the love of the game? Players worked hard and frequently came from a working class background, but perhaps they were not cut from the same entrepreneurial cloth as Sugar himself.

Whether you believe that players who rise early each morning to undergo exhausting training sessions can be considered in the same breath as the young Sugar, boiling beetroots at dawn and working hard all his life or not, nobody can deny that he sets a fine example for the people of Britain at any time, most of all during the credit crunch era. He has earned all the rewards that came from his work, but ask Sugar what really matters and he will not mention work, profit or success. Only one thing really matters to him when push comes to shove: his family.

CHAPTER THREE
FAMILY VALUES AND LOYALTY

Ask Sugar what the secret of his success is and his reply will be succinct: 'Put your loved ones, not your profit margin, centre-stage.' Lord Sugar has always been a family man, but where did his burning sense of family loyalty come from? Where was it born?

Although the household Sugar grew up in was not excessively religious, his formative years were spent in a definitely Jewish atmosphere. No wonder his sense of family loyalty is so strong: the family is central to Jewish culture and religion. In an era where family values find themselves regularly compromised and even attacked by modernist relativists, Sugar's unshakeable bond, love and loyalty with his nearest and dearest is refreshing.

His wealth might now set him aside from them in terms of bank balances, but he has always shared his success with his relatives and in the most appropriate of ways. Not for Sugar the condescending, ostentatious throwing around of money by the posturing rich relative – instead he has quietly invited them to join him in his success. From the start, his businesses have always had a family flavour to them. In return for his encouragement and generosity, his relatives have responded well. Most important, though, is that he has always been a loving husband, father, son and sibling.

His focus on the family has been as notable and admirable as has his ascent to financial fortune. This is a man who is rich in every sense, not merely a financial one.

His family values are all the more striking given that as a youngster he was in effect an only child, such was the distance in years between him and his siblings. The closest in age was 11 years his senior. He therefore had little in common with them as he grew up and was not overly welcome when he tried to tag along with them. His siblings, too, had been separated from the family in their own childhood, during World War II.

As Hackney, along with much of London, was bombed by the Germans, Fay and Nathan watched as Derek, Daphne and Shirley were evacuated to safety outside the city. The parents stayed in London and dodged the bombs by running to the air-raid shelter in the estate. The war was long over when Fay gave birth, after a long and complicated labour, to Alan on 24 March 1947. For the first years of his life, he was close to his family – particularly at night. He had to share a bedroom with

Daphne and Shirley until they left home. He was closest to Daphne, who took him under her wing, keeping an eye on him as he grew up. It was a relationship at times closer to mother and son than sister and brother, but it worked for them.

On a Friday night the family would gather round the table for a game of cards, often the trick game Solo. Nathan was a particular fan of cards. Alan was too young at first to join in but would sit or stand at the table, watching the game and noting how it brought the family together. Indeed, much of the socialising the family did was behind closed doors in their own home. Thus were the family bonds strengthened and Sugar learned the joys of a tight family unit. It may not have been entirely the traditional Jewish 'Friday night' Shabbat experience, but it was still playing true to the family-orientated heart of Judaism.

Nearby in the East End of London there were families with absent fathers, sometimes because the fathers were behind bars. True, Nathan had a temper at times but the Sugar household was one of a loving family that taught Sugar how to create such a bonded atmosphere in his adulthood. The Sugar boys went through the Bar Mitzvah ceremony when they turned 13. Sugar's took place at a small synagogue in Clapton Road, east London. (He would later marry in a synagogue, too – in Great Portland Street in London's West End.) As he memorably told a contestant on *The Apprentice*, 'I was in the Jewish Lads Brigade, Stamford Hill Division, trainee bugler.' So it was a Jewish childhood that he enjoyed, but perhaps one that focused more on secular Jewish culture than on any overtly religious side.

As his riches have grown, Sugar has been at pains to share the benefits with his beloved parents. A key example of this was when he decided it was time he helped them move to a finer home. He had plenty of money, so for him to help out was a no-brainer. It is a sentiment shared by many, in all financial situations. The punter buying a lottery ticket on a Saturday afternoon often dreams of wealth not just for him or herself but also for the chance to share it with their loved ones. Few wonder whether such an offer would be anything but gleefully accepted.

As it turned out, Sugar had to spend several years persuading Fay and Nathan to allow him to buy even a new flat for them. He felt the Hackney one they lived in was not appropriate or befitting of them, and he was keen to use his wealth to purchase a more spacious, comfortable property for them in nicer surroundings. He had his eye on a particular property in Redbridge, a London borough in the town of Ilford, but at first his urgings were in vain. The master salesman of the business world suddenly hit a brick wall of stern resistance as he found his own parents hard to convince – and he was offering to give, not sell, them something. Eventually they succumbed and allowed him to move them to a more comfortable environment.

It was not the only time that Sugar found it hard to convince his parents to let him treat them: it was much the same story with travel and leisure. Sugar was keen to give his parents relaxing holidays around the world, including Israel and America. Again, money was not the problem. He could comfortably afford to fly them first-class and to put them up in top hotels. However, due to understandable parental pride, they were uncomfortable with his offers. This time he found another way of convincing them: ever the canny operator, he would let them think that he had obtained the tickets and accommodation as freebies from his business contacts. Only then would they accept the trips. Sugar was just pleased to see them taking a well-deserved holiday and was glad to have been able to provide the very best facilities for them. Their sojourns overseas were glorious times for his parents, who finally allowed themselves to enjoy the luxury.

This was not the only way that he ensured his parents benefited from his extraordinary success. Sugar's employment of his sons in his businesses is well known. What is not so commonly told is that he employed his father from the early days of his business empire in the 1970s. As we have seen, Nathan worked in the garment trade and was slaving long hours in sweatshops for modest pay. Not only that, he faced the ever-present threat of unemployment due to the fickle nature of that industry. This was the precarious way of life that Sugar had observed as a child and which had been a major factor in pushing him to never follow such a lead. As an adult, it still broke Sugar's heart to see his own father in such a position, so he quickly brought him under the wing of Amstrad with a small job in the company.

Here it was that Sugar set his 'family affair' vision in place. Not that this was some moment of indulgent nepotism. The job he had given his father was one he was suited for and was not a senior one by any standards. 'He was earning something like £20 a week,' Sugar told David Thomas of his father's salary in the garment trade. 'The way I was doing business, twenty quid a week was nothing. So he might as well come and work for me and answer my telephones and wrap a few parcels up.'

Nathan was, reports Sugar, 'happy' to be working at Amstrad. He was, though, paranoid that his son's growing business would suddenly collapse. It was not unheard of for traders in the market near the Amstrad headquarters in Ridley Road to see Nathan scouring the pavement for discarded pieces of string. He would gather up all the string and return to Amstrad where he would deposit it in the stationary cupboard, ready to be used for tying up parcels. Likewise, he would steam postage stamps off envelopes and use them for Amstrad's outgoing mail. Sugar was both amused and exasperated by this. He would tell his father that the mail he was using the steamed-off stamps on included invoices for tens of thousands of pounds. As such, the saving made on the stamp was insignificant really.

Sugar senior would also interrupt meetings at Amstrad to tell his son that he had managed to get a good deal on some 'lovely oranges' at the local market. Such anecdotes might seem to put father and son at odds. However, many successful entrepreneurs have a very tight streak in them. So Nathan's behaviour was not entirely at odds with many of those who populate the rich lists. It took a long time for Sugar's parents to accept his wealth and that the entire empire was not about to collapse like a house of cards at a moment's notice. The risks and punts that Sugar had to take to climb up the business ladder were the sort of thing that terrified them. It was not that they did not want him to succeed, nor that they lacked faith in their son. It was just that, like most people, they had never witnessed such determination and ambition, so they viewed it all not so much with suspicion as trepidation.

Right from the time Sugar obtained his first Vauxhall Viva van in the 1960s, he came face-to-face with his father's neurosis. Sugar was all set to sign a hire purchase agreement for the van, but was too young legally to enter into such an agreement. He asked his father if he would put his name on the form. Sugar would then pay the instalments himself. However, Nathan was so concerned about his son's future that he worried about his son being in debt to the hire firm and paid the money himself. His son would be in debt only to him. 'It was the typical mentality of my father,' said Sugar. 'He couldn't understand that I'd ever be able to pay the money back.'

Sugar also employed his brother Derek for a while in the early 1970s, as a stock supervisor. It was a short-term employment and Derek was soon back driving taxis. It was a career choice he'd taken after having been removed from school at 14 by his father and sent straight to work in the garment trade as a machinist. Some would view this as a shame. Derek had been a very promising pupil at school and was naturally very bright. He hated the monotony of the work in the rag-trade and became a cab driver. Who can know whether, had he stayed longer at school – as he'd wished to – there might have been better opportunities for him in life? One can only speculate how different his life might have been.

Nathan allowed Alan to stay at school until he was 16. The boy wanted to remain longer but his father felt he had already compromised enough in allowing him to stay on so long and he left shortly before his 17th birthday.

He then continued on the path to becoming a businessman which he had started in his spare time at school. For Nathan, a man who had worked so hard in his life and always in the employ of others, his son's career path was puzzling. This clash of mentalities was not easily resolved and it took an ongoing and lengthy campaign by Sugar to convince his father to relax.

'It wasn't until I physically put a cheque for £2 million under his nose that he realised it was OK for him to stop worrying because I actually could make a living without working for somebody.' For Sugar, as we shall see, the most important thing was that his riches should benefit his family. He did not spoil his own children; rather he gave them a start in life. However cynical one may be about nepotism, there is surely nothing about the way he has employed his children that is anything other than touching.

Take the way he has used his son Daniel in various projects. Daniel had been thrown in at the deep end from an early age. Having left school at 16 he went straight to work in the marketing department of Amstrad. It was an interesting first day in the office for the teenager. His father took him to see the head of marketing, Thomas Power, and snapped: 'This is Daniel. This is my son. I want you to teach him all that marketing crap you lot go on about down here. I want you to teach him everything you know. If he gives you any talk-back, send him up to me. And if he doesn't do what you tell him, throw him out the door.'

There was no need for such action, for Power was soon impressed with young Sugar. 'He's got the bolshy, "Oh, yeah, I'm a trader, I'm a banana salesman and I'll sell you a satellite dish on the side" attitude,' said the marketing manager with approval.

No wonder Sugar went on to give his son such a prominent role in Amsair, the successful private jet hire company Sugar formed in 1993: he was just the man to watch over the development of the many services that Amsair offers its clients. 'We are set up rather differently from most private jet companies,' explains Sugar junior. 'The aircraft are brand new. We offer pretty much a concierge service for private clients. We look after every detail from the moment a client has booked.' This is no small detail, but rather a fundamental selling point for Amsair that distinguishes it from much of the competition. Food is just one example of how Amsair can personally tailor its service to demand, as Daniel explains. 'Clients may want a meal ordered from somewhere else and we'll organise that. We'll also be flight-tracking to check for any possible delays and we'll triple check the car transfers at either end of the journey.'

For some, however, Sugar's employment of his relatives is not the sign of a loving and trusting father. Although his hiring of his offspring has invariably been vindicated, some will always sniff an air of cosiness. For instance, the sneering City Spy column in the *Evening Standard* reported that *Apprentice* candidates were given a task of producing an advertisement. The writers found this all far too convenient.

'The product they advertise is a booking card for Amsair, Sugar's executive jet business,' it reported. 'It is run by his son, Daniel, who makes his debut on the programme. What's that? You thought Sir Alan was a tough-minded meritocrat?'

Let the cynics have their say. Meanwhile, Daniel continues to prove his worth on the frontline for Amsair. In the dark financial climate of recent times, luxuries such as private jets have often been the first things to disappear from company and individual budgets. It's the treats that are axed first and a private jet is firmly in that camp. Daniel saw this trend coming and did his best to adapt. 'We are mindful of the fact that the economy isn't marvellous at the moment and as it's a competitive industry we can't be too expensive. We are not going after huge turnover. We have long-standing clients – about 60 to 70 of them – but they come back to us because we don't let them down. We run a lean machine and are clear in what we offer.'

Daniel showed that he had inherited plenty of his father's business acumen from an early age. He enterprisingly booked a hall in Essex on the night that Sky televised the Mike Tyson v Frank Bruno fight and charged people £30 a head to watch the fight and eat a meal. It turned out to be a nice little earner for Daniel, then just 18. Later, with his business skills underscored, he was made 'head of operations' at Tottenham Hotspur in the latter years of his father's tenure at the club. 'I don't think it makes a difference to my position who my father is. We agree on the objectives we are trying to achieve here,' he said. 'We want Spurs to be in a position to win things over the next few years.'

He was affected by the bitter personal attacks on his father by some Spurs fans. 'I don't think it would have been normal not to have been hurt by the personal criticism of my father, especially when you think it is unjustified,' he said. Although his father found he sometimes had to protect his son, the experience toughened Daniel up. 'Now I am involved in the football club I have come to accept that, if you are in this business, you are going to get that type of criticism, whether it is justified or not.' As a long-term Spurs fan, Daniel was delighted to be given a chance to serve the club. He had attended FA Cup Finals the club had competed in and had even bunked school to watch matches. Daniel even got to pull on the famous kit himself when a 'Spurs XI' took on a team of financial journalists in 1999.

Sugar also gave his son Simon a break in business. Simon had been born the same year as Amstrad was formed and he would benefit from the firm in his adulthood. When he left school he took an internship-style position at Dixons in order to gain a good understanding of the company's workings and customers. He was stationed at a key store in central London. 'He wanted to learn retailing and he did,' said Stanley Kalms, chairman of Dixons. 'He is a very quiet, hardworking and modest lad. He was treated just like anyone else – well, just like anyone else who had Alan Sugar for a father. I'm sure he was treated nicer than he should have been but it wasn't company policy.'

But Dixons was not the first taste of working life that Simon had had – his first job was at McDonalds. Hardly the opening gambit of a man benefiting from cushy nepotism, is it?

Later, Sugar gave Simon another break in the form of a

role in the running of his infamous 'E-mailer' product. 'Business is business and family is family and the two things are kept completely separate with us,' said Simon, who joined at the age of 26. 'He treats me like any other employee and that's how it should be.' Again, for some, all this was too good to be true and the press made sneering remarks about the arrangement. One newspaper, for instance, described Simon as 'a trust fund kid'.

Simon sold his shares in Amstrad in December 2005, in the wake of a painful divorce. Some speculated it was in the anticipation of a hefty settlement fee being needed; others wondered if this marked a vote of no-confidence in the company from the owner's own son. Simon was quick to dismiss the latter concern. 'This sale of my shares in the company has been done purely for personal reasons and should not be construed as a reflection of my views on the prospects for the company or my intention to remain as a director of the company,' he said.

Sugar's daughter Louise is a director of his property company Amsprop, having also worked for Amstrad. She protests strongly against claims that anything has come her way easily. For instance, she says, as a child she would have to stand at the foot of her parents' bed each Saturday and build a winning case for her to receive her weekly pocket money. Since then she has worked hard for her father's companies and subsequently enjoyed the trappings of her success, driving a sports car with a personalised number plate.

In the autumn of 1995 she embarked on a romance with Darren Dein, the son of then Arsenal supremo David Dein. Given her father's chairmanship of Arsenal's bitter rivals Tottenham and Louise's support for Spurs it was a headline-grabbing relationship. They met in the Arsenal boardroom after a north London derby. 'She's grown very fond of Darren – we could even see her in an Arsenal top soon,' a friend told the press. The romance did not last, however.

She met another future partner at a football match too. Mark Baron was once a member of the boy band Another Level and his path crossed Louise's at a match between Tottenham and Wimbledon. They quickly hit it off but the relationship did not blossom until they met again in a nightclub some time later. They got engaged in the spring of 2000, when he took her to Venice and popped the question on one of the city's famous gondolas.

'My bottom lip quivered and very quickly I said, "Yes, definitely",' she said.

'We're both extremely happy, as are both sets of parents,' Mark told the press as they set a date for the summer of 2001. It capped a gloriously happy time for Louise, coming the same summer as her father's knighthood. 'This has been one of the best periods of my life – I'm almost waiting for the bubble to burst,' she told *Hello!* magazine.

No wonder Sugar is so proud of his children, and so he should be, for he has shared his success with them in the most fitting of ways. 'I wanted them to see how the rest of the world live, to realise they have a privileged life,' he said. 'I think they are all fairly well-balanced. Ann and I wanted them to grow up with the same values that we had. I figure once they've got past a certain stage and they're not out beating up old ladies then you've won. They are really down-to-earth, nice people, don't sling their weight around. They've never been the Ferrari-driving, cocaine-sniffing, party-going type. They've got the right values.'

Sugar has not just been a loyal son and father, but also a devoted husband. A radio panel show once asked the contestants to name the worst possible life. 'Being married to Alan Sugar' came an answer. Ann would doubtless disagree.

'She's the complete opposite to me,' he said. 'She never cared about money. She just wanted the family to be comfortable.'

Alan met Ann back in 1966, when their paths crossed due to their membership of the youth clubs of Stamford Hill. When he strolled into one such club one summer evening, Ann was enchanted by the swaggering young man. The first thing she noticed about him was, she said, 'his manners – there weren't many. Alan's not the romantic type. Definitely not, never has been. He was very straight-talking and I wasn't used to that type of thing at all. But that's what I liked about him.'

As soon as they met, Sugar soon fell for the trainee hairdresser, then called Ann Simons. She was shy but beautiful. She was also swiftly impressed by him, though she admits that he was something of an oddity in her eyes due to his incessant focus on work. 'He was completely different from anybody else I had ever met,' she said. 'He wanted to work all the time. He wasn't like an ordinary 18-year-old boy.' All the same, or perhaps because of his uniqueness, she was quickly enamoured of Sugar. It was as close to love at first sight as happens in the real world. Not that the course of true love was going to be trodden easily by the couple, for opposition to their courtship was just round the corner.

Ann's family was not at all impressed by their daughter's choice of partner. For her part she enjoyed sitting alongside him as he worked on his latest deliveries and would happily read a book as he loaded and unloaded the van. The family viewed the somewhat rough and ready Sugar as being far from their dream son-in-law. And they were vocal in their opposition, as Gulu Lalvani, the chairman of an electronics company that Sugar did business with, discovered one day. Ann's father Johnny was a customer of his company and took him to one side for a chat one day. 'He was very angry,' recalls Lalvani. 'He said, "See that young man? Tell him I don't want him to go out with my daughter." I told him that he had to tell him on his own. Johnny was a good customer. He wanted his daughter to marry a lawyer or a doctor. I told him Alan was a good customer and I couldn't say that kind of thing to him.'

Alan Sugar at
the Brentwood
headquarters of
Amstrad.

Above: The appointment of George Graham as manager of Tottenham was to prove a controversial one for Sugar.

Below: The Tottenham fans had a fiery relationship with chairman Sugar.

Left: The E-Mailer phone was launched in 1999 but was not to be one of the best-performing products for Amstrad.

Right: Chancellor Gordon Brown and Sugar toured the country as part of a drive to promote the qualities of enterprise which motivated the success of world-beating companies like Amstrad.

Above: A collection of multi-millionaires in Downing Street. Sugar with Prime Minister Tony Blair, Richard Branson and EasyJet's Stelios Haji-Ioannou.

Below: An evening at the Hackney Empire with support from the Sugar clan.

Above: *The Apprentice* line-up in 2007 – Margaret Mountford, Sugar and Nick Hewer. *Inset*: Karren Brady would take over from Mountford for the 2010 series.

Below: Sugar watches his health through his passion for cycling and, *inset*, his personalised bike.

Left: Ann has often been credited by Sugar for playing a key part in his success.

Right: Sugar continued to maintain his relationship with Gordon Brown after the former Chancellor became Prime Minister.

Left: 'You're furred!'
The newest Lord on the
block makes his way to
hear the Queen's speech
to Parliament.

Right: Despite his sometimes
troubled relationship with his
team, Lord Sugar continues
to support Tottenham as they
play Wigan Athletic in
November 2009.

Top: Jonathan Ross's chat show provided a platform for Sugar's ready wit.

Middle: The unmistakeable shape of Sugar's Rolls-Royce pulls out of Downing Street.

Left: In late 2009, enterprise champion Lord Sugar appeared at the British Library to give advice to the next generation.

As Lalvani later told David Thomas, this opposition was not going to be enough to put Sugar off. 'It motivated him even more. He wanted to prove to his girlfriend's father that, OK, he might not be a doctor or an accountant or a lawyer, but he could be a successful businessman.'

Indeed, Sugar felt he was learning a whole new way of working life by rubbing shoulders with different people, including her family. 'I met a different class of person,' he recalled. 'Some of their parents were in business and I saw a little bit of a different way of life.'

Soon the Simons were won round to their daughter's choice of man and the couple got engaged, marrying in 1968 at the Great Portland Street synagogue. The service was followed by a grand bash in the West End. As a family friend of Sugar told the *Mail on Sunday*, the opposition to the couple's relationship was now a thing of the past. 'The families put on a good show at the wedding – a clear sign that the Simons were reconciled to Ann's choice. It was a very joyous occasion and both families seemed to get on just fine.'

The newly married couple bought their first home together in Redbridge. It was a semi-detached, wide-windowed house on Marlands Road in a district called Clayhall, a relatively nice area full of semi-detached houses and even a few grand mock Tudor properties. Indeed, the location was significant and symbolic: it was not far from where Ann's parents lived and was thus an early sign to them that their new son-in-law might have

145

come from what they considered the wrong side of the tracks, but he had no intention of staying there.

Ann was made a director of Amstrad in the 1970s and Sugar was to make sure the Simons' daughter had the most comfortable of lives. In 1972 they moved to a new house in Chigwell Rise on the border of Essex and London. Here they had even posher neighbours and expensive cars sat in the driveways of every house on the long street.

The work/home division between the couple is clearly laid out. 'Work-wise, Alan does what he wants,' says Ann. 'But in the house, I'm in charge – and he quite likes it that way.'

Sugar never moans at her about how is working life is going, he insists. 'No, because I know she would not have anything to offer me other than telling me to stop worrying.' He once gave himself plenty to worry about when he accidentally made a major faux pas on his wife's birthday. He only remembered at the last minute that it was Ann's big day, and called Louise to his office, asking her to go and buy a suitable card. The card was bought and placed by Sugar's secretary onto a pile of papers for him to sign. He raced through the papers and not noticing that the card was for his wife, signed it: 'Best wishes, Alan Sugar'.

When Ann opened the card, she was appalled. However, the couple tell differing stories as to what happened next. 'She just looked at me,' claimed Sugar, rolling his eyes and making a 'tut' sound, 'like that, as if to say, yeah, thoughtless person.'

The way Ann tells it, she was not quite so calm. 'I was furious with him, absolutely furious,' she said. 'I can't remember my exact words, but he knew I was very annoyed.'

As we have seen, Sugar plays hard just as he works hard. However, one of his playthings was enough to give Ann plenty to worry about. In the 1970s Sugar felt obliged to respond when his wife put her foot down over his flying hobby. By this time he had taken to flying to meetings across the UK. He enjoyed it, felt it meant that he arrived in style and could also shave hours off his journey time by avoiding Britain's busy roads and, at times, crippled rail network. He had passed both his standard flying test and the more advanced ones that test a pilot's ability in extreme weather conditions. He'd bought himself a single-engine plane for £7,500 and flew it around England and even overseas. He loved to fly while on holiday, collecting an American licence during one holiday in the Catskill Mountains, and also took to the air over Hawaii. Glorious days for him as he celebrated his success in the most uplifting way.

But during one flight back from France he had a close shave, enough to terrify Ann when she heard the details. While he was in the skies over the Channel, he noticed that something seemed not right with the plane. However, he managed to land safely at Southend, where he was to pass through customs before flying off again.

As he took off, he described the engine as 'crocked'. He was in big trouble. His plane was over Southend town centre and he had to make an emergency landing in fields to avoid the busy area.

The problem was that one of the cylinders had broken and he kept the offending component in his office as a – rather grizzly – memento for many years. Ann, who had been concerned about his new hobby, now urged him to stop. Sugar's response was to switch to a twin-engine plane, which offered more safety. However, he found these models were not as much fun as the single-engine equivalents. 'It really took the fun out of flying,' he complained. So, with Ann pressing him to stop flying altogether, he decided to hang up his flying goggles. For the time being, at least.

He replaced flying with a new pastime – tennis. As we have seen, he has used this to great charitable effect. All the same, the fact that he had taken up flying as a hobby was evidence that he was moving up in the world socially. With his new-found riches he was enjoying fine holidays and living in very comfortable surroundings. He did not let it change him, though. 'I know where my roots are,' he said. 'My family are still working-class people.'

Sugar returned to flying later in life and had another drama that caused concern for his family and friends. He was trying to land his four-seat Cirrus SR20 near Manchester on a wet and thundery day. 'We landed at Barton, a friendly and club-like airfield now named City

Airport Manchester – a far grander name than it suggests with a grass runway about the same length as a football pitch,' recalled Sugar. 'We landed and ran over the end of the slippery runway by about 15 feet into some taller grass. In doing so the propeller of the plane picked up some minor damage and according to the rules this means the plane can't fly unless checked out by a qualified engineer.'

The authorities arrived and towed the plane by tractor to a hangar. If Sugar and his passenger were concerned they had a funny way of showing it: they returned to the airport clubhouse and tucked into some food.

He later laughed off the reported danger. 'As far as "life-threatening" is concerned, to put things in perspective my friend and I had as much chance of dying from the incident as we did of dying from food poisoning from the tuna sandwich that a very nice lady made us in the clubhouse while we waited for a mate to pick us up and take us home.'

Another pilot present at the airfield said: 'He made the final approach a little bit quick and because of the rain and the state of the runway couldn't stop the aeroplane. He wasn't shaken or hurt but he seemed quite annoyed with himself. It is only a small airport. There is not a great deal of room for pilot error. Had he been going much faster, it could have been a very different story.'

Sugar's spokesman tried to play the incident down. 'The accident was due to the weather being particularly wet and heavy,' the spokesman told the *Daily Mail*. 'It is also a very short runway. For Sir Alan this was just a pleasure trip. He flies a great deal at the weekends.'

As they became richer, the Sugars did their best to introduce their growing wealth to their relatives in the most appropriate way. In the 1980s, they moved to a mightily impressive property, walking distance from their Chigwell Rise home but worlds away in every other sense. It was in an area where millionaires lived and as such it was an impressive home indeed, an L-shaped property set in a large garden. It even had its own roof terrace. The large house was set in large grounds and it was a memorable day when his family first came to visit.

Sugar's sister Daphne had been warned by Ann to expect a very impressive sight, but when she and her husband Harold pulled up in their car they were stunned. So stunned that they had to drive back and forwards in front of the property before they parked and knocked on the door. 'We couldn't believe the size of the property,' she remembered. 'We'd never seen anything like that.' Daphne remembers her parents being shocked as well. 'When my mother and father first went to see it, they were totally confused. They couldn't take it in. They just hadn't realised how big Alan had got.'

However big Alan gets, he remains in awe of his wife. 'Ann is respected by everyone,' he said with pride. 'She is the opposite of me but we complement each other and she can read me like a book. She knows when I have a lot on my mind and is happy to let me sit watching TV while I wind down. Sometimes when I get home on a Friday night my head is still pounding with the problems of the week.'

As a friend explained, their marriage works like clockwork because they fit together so well. 'They made a pact very early on in their relationship that Ann would stay at home and look after the family while he would take care of building up the business. Ann is a very bright woman and could easily have made a career for herself. She used to help out in the early days when they ran the business at home, but Alan is a highly moral man and wanted a strong sense of morality instilled in the children when they were growing up.

'The only person he trusted to do this was Ann. In fact he probably wouldn't even have gone out to work unless he'd known she was at home overseeing everything there. In other words, she created the stability and classic Jewish home life which he needed behind him. This in turn gave him the strength and peace of mind he needed to go out and be a successful businessman. She's more modern matriarch than classic Jewish matriarch. She's always very well turned-out but far from glamorous. She's not the type to flaunt the family wealth and is not a regular at Harrods or anything like that. She's very much the family's anchor and Alan's personal anchor. They are still very close and loving with each other which adds to Alan's strength as a businessman.'

It is a circular relationship: just as his business success has helped his family, so Sugar's family values have long benefited his business. Some of his earliest contracts and breaks in business came as a result of the close-knit ties that existed within the Jewish community in London at the time. Families were close and looked out for one another, and Sugar was ready to cash in. His first accountant was Guy Gordon, Ann's cousin. He offered fine advice to Sugar, among which was a way to avoid putting his home in danger if his company were to run into financial trouble.

Then Sugar made friends with Ashley Morris, whose wife was the first cousin of his sister's husband. The two became fathers at the same time in 1969, Sugar for the first time. As the wives attended ante-natal classes together, the husbands became friends and would dine out together, discussing business. Before long they went into business, selling audio equipment. But each had his own idea of how one got on in business.

'I don't care what you say, Alan,' said Morris, 'success in business is 50 per cent hard work and 50 per cent luck. You have to have the luck running with you otherwise you get nowhere.'

Sugar was having none of this. 'No, mate, it's hard work,' he said 'It's all hard work.'

Alan Sugar has been painfully honest about how he feels he has done well to marry, and stay married, to a woman as beautiful as Ann. Where some businessmen preen and delude themselves about their own level of attractiveness, he has never kidded himself nor tried to kid anyone else. Not that he is without sex appeal. Kate Walsh, runner-up in the 2009 series of *The Apprentice*, has said that she believes he has – for the right people – a definite charm. 'For a certain age, he would have sex appeal,' she told *Now* magazine. The beautiful blonde, now a television presenter on Five, added: 'He's definitely got a bit of a twinkle in his eye.' Not that she holds a candle for him: 'I'm not a fan of the older man,' she said. Indeed, as viewers saw, she was more enamoured by fellow contestant Phillip Taylor.

Sugar is a fan of Walsh – for her business acumen. He told her, she claims, that he had wanted to hire her along with the series winner Yasmina Siadatan but was prevented from doing so by BBC rules which state he must only hire the series winner. Interestingly, Sugar has said that he keeps his decision as to who has won secret from everybody – including Ann. She gives him, he says, 'a bit of grief' about this decision. '[She says] "You can trust me, I've married you for 42 years, let me know!" … I said, "No," because she might tell the greengrocer.'

In one area of family, however, Sugar has views that attract controversy and unpleasant headlines. He has spoken out against the 1975 legislation which banned employers from asking potential female employees at interview whether they are pregnant or plan to become so. 'It's got to such a state now that you can't ask the obvious questions,' he complained when the law changed. His conclusion: 'Just don't employ them. It will get harder to get a job as a woman.' Expanding on his theme, he said: 'Everything has gone too far. We have maternity laws where people are entitled to too much. If someone comes into an interview and you think to yourself, There is a possibility that this woman might have a child and therefore take time off, it is a bit of a psychological negative thought.

'If they are applying for a position which is very important then I should imagine that some employers might think, This is a bit risky. They would like to ask the question: "Are you planning to get married and to have any children?"'

He was not without support as – mostly anonymous – small business owners hit cyberspace to voice their sympathy with Sugar's view. 'It is high time someone of high profile said what every employer is scared to say: "I would not employ women" ... The reason I do not employ women is that I run a small business and there is no way that I could fund maternity benefits.'

Another said: 'I know where you are coming from as we too are the same ... If we do look for a female staff member, we would want somebody in her late forties or early fifties.'

Sugar also received on-the-record support in the *Daily Mail* from writer Katie Grant. 'The problem for women is not men in general and particularly not men like Sir Alan,' she wrote. 'Rather, it is increasingly those women who have failed to realise that the gender wars of the

1970s are over. While answering questions about having babies may be uncomfortable ... they are perhaps even more disadvantaged by the kind of battleground rhetoric old-guard feminists favour. Such rhetoric might once have been necessary but it is now managing to destroy something even more essential to good male/female working relations than equality, and that is trust. Taking on an employee involves time and expense, particularly in a small firm. So it seems not only reasonable but possibly helpful to discuss what the future may hold.'

She concluded rousingly, 'The stark truth is, however, that in many ways Sir Alan's observations have more point than the Sex and Power report [by the Equality and Human Rights Commission] and if old-school feminists want to be part of the modern world, they'll just have to get over it.'

Claire Byrne of the *Sunday Tribune* agreed: 'While the idealists have lamented his statement as a retrograde step for women's rights, realists know that he is right, but almost all are afraid to admit it.'

Naturally, he received a dressing-down from plenty of other writers. As a man who has been outspoken and brusque for as long as anyone can remember, he was natural prey for the pens of the press. 'Women have a right nerve, don't they?' wrote Lindsay Clydesdale in the *Daily Record*. Oozing sarcasm, she continued: 'First they get pregnant, then they want maternity pay and then the lazy cows expect their job to still be there for them when they return after up to a year of leave. During which time, we all know they're not sleep-deprived, lonely and exhausted but living it up at home on an extended holiday. Thank goodness then that Sir Alan Sugar, the snarling face of *The Apprentice*, has found the balls to speak up for all the put-upon millionaire businessmen out there, who're being bled dry by feckless females.'

Clydesdale continued in this vein for some time, concluding, 'The reality for women in the 21st century, where two thirds of mums in employment have to work so they can afford to eat, must terrify an old dinosaur like Sir Alan. Refusing to employ women would wipe out half the UK's workforce and push millions into poverty – not his best idea then. Time for a lie-down, Sir Alan, you're tired.' Well, at least this was a more novel take on using the old 'you're fired' line.

Some responses to his agenda were more nuanced, however. In the wake of his comments, feminist pioneer and newspaper legend Rosie Boycott proposed a third way: give *both* men and women the same length of parental leave. 'Then you would take away the fear of the employer thinking, I won't have the woman because it's the woman who'll want to go. That comment Alan Sugar made about tearing up the CV of a woman was absolutely shocking. But that's where we've got to and it's a tragic state of affairs.'

Part of the problem with this controversy is that his detractors can pull out a number of contentious remarks from his archives. He has also said: 'Women working together can sometimes be very difficult with each other: they can have lots of backbiting and jockeying for position.' Together, these quotes can form a drip-drip case against him, especially when they are quoted out of context. In the wake of the debate that such comments threw up, Sugar decided to clarify matters as best he could. He wrote a wide-ranging article in the *Mirror* which he hoped would dampen the fury and make clear his true position.

'The reason this is such a big issue is that there is an illusion that all employers are the size of major brands. Companies like BP or Tesco have thousands of employees and back-up in case someone is unable to work. The reality is that the backbone of the economy is made up of small- to medium-size businesses which employ from 10 to 100 people. And with these, every member of staff is vital to the success of the company. These smaller companies are well-oiled machines with no spare parts – the boss employs exactly the staff they need. They are not a charity and people are employed to do a job and be part of the team. A well-run small company is like a car engine. Without the carburettor, the car would conk out. So it's important that these employers have workers they can rely on to be there. Things need to run smoothly, without constant absences. I know this is not fair but business doesn't always do fair. Women have to accept this reality and be shrewd enough to deal with it.'

Apprentice winner Michelle Dewberry was disheartened by some of Sugar's words, but also urges we keep perspective from all sides. 'If you ask people what their views are on pregnancy, how far will you take it? Will you ask them about their menstrual cycle? Will you ask them about period pain? Or whether they have endometriosis? Where do you draw the line? Women didn't choose to be the gender that carries babies and we shouldn't be penalised.'

Dewberry denies, though, that Lord Sugar is anti-women in his opinions, as alleged by Cath Elliot in the *Guardian*, who has described him as 'a sexist dinosaur'. 'To say he's sexist is not right – otherwise how could he have ended up with two women at the finals?' she observes. 'I think Alan just needs to advance his management style a little and realise that you can get a whole lot more from people if you develop flexibility in the way you treat them.'

Others remain to be convinced. Karen Bremner was an *Apprentice* contestant in 2006 and was sceptical and disparaging of Sugar, particularly in his treatment of women. '[He] has made no secret of his feelings about women in business,' she said. 'He sees nothing wrong in asking about their plans for a family and how they would arrange childcare provision. Some commentators have suggested that he may even be scared of strong women. The truth, I fear, is much more simple. I don't think he really gets women.' Bremner's assertion is weakened by the presence of several strong women around Sugar. However, the former contestant actually tries to use this evidence against her assertion to prove its merit.

'He likes his women quiet, demure and feminine. Even the rock-solid Margaret speaks only when spoken to and has become increasingly girly as the series have gone on. Karren Brady, another force to be reckoned with, is a favourite of Sugar. She may have balls of steel but they are tempered with a soft voice and pretty clothes. Michelle Dewberry managed to fool him into thinking she would slip quietly into his organisation as she made plans for her escape and her own business,' she claims.

Coming to a rousing conclusion, she turned on Sugar hugely. 'Sugar thinks women who have opinions are trouble. He thinks they will be difficult to manage. He thinks demure equals malleable. So what do you have to do to make it in business as a woman? If you want to work for Alan Sugar, wear pink, smile a lot and don't raise your voice above a whisper.'

These words do not just insult Sugar, they are also a major slur on the integrity of the many women he has worked alongside in his career. Indeed, given the intelligence, wit and strength of character that is evident in Margaret Mountford, it seems unlikely that she would put up with any sexist behaviour from Sugar. Her views on women in the workplace are clear and pronounced. Had Sugar expressed similar views he would no doubt face more accusations of sexism. Mountford's endorsement of them suggests otherwise. She has spoken out against the introduction of a quota system to get more women on the board of directors of big companies.

'If you think you only get on a board because 50 per cent of people have to be women, what self respect can you have?' she asked passionately. 'You're just there to make up the numbers. Women should stick at it, hang on in there. In the professions, certainly, women can get to the top. But they don't always want to. You can't complain that you are not on the board if you decide you want to leave the mainstream, have a few years off, then come back and not work the hours. They want companies to bend over backwards. If they are talented enough people will want them, but why should companies be forced to have them? I don't approve of positive discrimination.'

The controversy proves groundless the more one looks into it. In November 2009 a law suit against Lord Sugar from a former female employee was dropped. Hanna Sebright had been planning to sue Sugar, his son Simon, *Apprentice* winner Lee McQueen and another Amstrad employee. Sebright was the founder of Electronic Health Media Limited, which sells advertising space on digital information screens in schools and hospitals. It was taken over by Lord Sugar and taken under the Amscreen umbrella. She was reported to be seeking £140,000 in compensation for sexual discrimination and constructive unfair dismissal, but she abandoned the action in 2009.

David Fraser of Franks PR represents Sugar and said, 'Hanna Sebright, a former employee of Amscreen Group Limited, of which Lord Sugar was chairman until 1 July 2009, has withdrawn all claims raised in London East employment tribunal against Amscreen and the four individual named respondents, including Lord Sugar. In particular, Ms Sebright now accepts that the claims she raised against Lord Sugar in his personal capacity were entirely without foundation.'

Theresa May, the shadow equalities minister, was still keen to question Sugar's attitude, though. 'He is a person I have taken issue with in the past for his, if I am kind, somewhat old-fashioned views on women in the workplace,' she said during a speech on women in business in December 2009.

Sugar described Mrs May's comments as 'absolute rubbish'. He added that Mrs May 'has never met me or even taken the opportunity to question or confront me on these matters. Instead it seems she forms her opinions by what she reads in papers and, just like those articles, it means she is also not to be trusted.'

Let us close on a happier note, with more evidence of Sugar's love and devotion to his wife Ann. On their 40th wedding anniversary he put on a seriously grand black-tie bash at the couple's Chigwell mansion. He spoke movingly of his love and admiration for Ann. 'I feel a bit of a fraud standing up here,' he told the guests during his speech. 'It is true that over the past 25 years or so, due to my various shenanigans, the focus of attention has been on me. Quite unfairly so, as behind me is Ann – someone who has always sat in the background and let it all happen. But she has been by my side through good and bad times – fortunately not too many bad times. Ann has been a great leveller for me, and kept me on the straight and level. She, of course, wanted me to succeed in whatever I have done, but I think most of you know that's not where her priorities are. Happy family life always came first, as well as the welfare of others.'

Moving words, but Sugar showed he can crack gags too. 'I can honestly say I have never ever heard anyone say a bad word about Ann,' he said. 'As you know, you can't say the same about me. Talk about chalk and cheese. She always says the day she met me she knew she had met Mr Right; what she didn't know was that my first name was Always.' He then turned to the notorious birthday card he had signed with the impersonal greeting. 'It was a busy day in the office,' he said, attempting to explain it to the audience. 'Ann was not a happy bunny. So I apologised and then ran through loads of things I could buy her to make up for my mistake.

'Do you want a new dress?'

'No.'

'A new watch?'

'No.'

'A car?'

'No.'

'OK, well, just tell me what I can get you…'

To which she replied, 'A bloody divorce!'

As laughter filled the room, Sir Alan added, 'I said, "Sorry, I wasn't thinking of spending that much."' The jokes were coming thick and fast. 'She ended up the next day buying me something that she said went from 0-20 in three seconds – a bloody set of bathroom scales.' By now, the laughter greeting his gags was rivalling that which had been forthcoming for Jackie Mason's hilarious set earlier in the evening.

'Last week, we were driving home from the airport, and Ann commented that it was 40 years to the day since we got married. To which I nodded, as you do when driving, and muttered, "Yeah amazing, eh?" Then there was a silence, as there is when you are driving along. A few moments later she said to me, "Do I see a tear in your eyes? Don't tell me you are going soft and feeling sentimental." I said, "I am going to tell you something now that I have never told you before. Forty years ago, your father took out his old army pistol, held it to my head and told me if I didn't marry you he would make sure I was banged up in jail for 40 years. So yeah, I am being sentimental – the thing is, I would be getting out tomorrow."'

Sir Alan always insisted that he not only puts his family before business but also that the only way to succeed in his field is to put it second to your loved ones. It was a message he repeated on the night. 'Now here is a message to those young aspiring men here tonight. I would remind you what it is to be a successful man and what is one's prized possession in life. It has absolutely nothing at all to do with money, academic achievement, or any material things. A real successful man puts the love of his wife and children first. A real successful man's greatest position in life is to have a great family. I am lucky enough to have had a wife for 40 years, who gave me three great children, who in turn have given us seven wonderful grandchildren. You see, everything I have today is because of the love of that lady and the respect my three children have for the both of us. Ladies and gentlemen, thank you for coming – let's have a great night.'

They did have a great night, as those present have heartily attested. But it was not just a one-off evening of joy for the happy couple: Lord Sugar and his wife enjoy a great marriage, too. 'Family and business: you want them both settled. A happy balance. I was brought up with true family values. We were poor but we had standards. And my wife Ann came from a similar background.'

In the wake of the 2009 series of *The Apprentice*, Sugar showed his class touch when assessing the media coverage of the series. Rarely a fan of journalists, he expressed his disappointment over how the show had been covered in the popular press. Throughout the series, he had picked up newspapers and read their stories about the latest goings-on in *Apprentice*-land. It had made unhappy reading for the tycoon. He had been mightily impressed by the candidates, but found that his feelings were not being reflected on the printed page. 'They've been a great bunch this year,' he said. 'The class of 2009 have been the best bunch I've ever had, to be honest with you.' Which made it all the more infuriating for him when they were mocked by what he saw as sneering journalists. 'What I'm going to do for the next series is: I'm not going to read the papers during the course of the transmission because people … they start having a go at the people and all that stuff and it really is annoying,' he said.

Warming to his theme, he showed his admiration for and loyalty towards the contestants by restating the challenges they faced. 'People don't seem to understand how difficult it is, the pressure that they're under, the circumstances that they're under,' he said. 'They keep taking the mickey out of a lot of people and I feel a bit unhappy about it sometimes.' It was not the first time that he had defended *Apprentice* contestants from media attack. When *Newsnight* presenter Jeremy Paxman said that the show was populated by 'know-alls' with 'nothing interesting to say', Sugar saw red and let rip.

'That's the pot talking to the kettle, isn't it?' he asked. 'I mean, he's the most unpleasant person going. I'd like to get into a debate, without him having a day to think up questions to make people seem awkward. I'd like to see how clever he is then.' He added, 'Jeremy Paxman has never interviewed me. I've never met him. But I'd like to be thrown in a room with him to debate something someone throws at us rather than him having a crib sheet hiding under the table. In my opinion that is cheating, honestly.'

Sugar's fairness towards the candidates is, says former series sidekick Mountford, heightened in his dealings with younger candidates. According to the ever-popular advisor, he is lenient towards those of more tender years. 'The youth thing – he does make allowances for people without the common sense, gravitas or moderation that some learn with years,' she said. He is also well-disposed towards those who had to fight from poverty. Mindful of his own humble background, he admires those with the drive to emerge from poverty. Not that, as we saw in the Honesty chapter, that means he is about to be biased towards them.

'He has a soft spot for those who've had a hard start,' Mountford revealed. 'But if someone who was brought up on one crust of bread a week, living in a cardboard box, makes a complete mess of things in task one, they are still going to go.'

Might we see a softer Sugar in future series of *The Apprentice*? We could have done, he says, in past editions of the show, if the BBC had edited it differently. He has always been keen for a more balanced picture to emerge of him on television. 'It's a continual argument I have with the production people,' he said. 'But like it or not, and I don't like it that much, there's a perception of me just banging the table and shouting.' With the leaner financial climate of recent times and his newfound political role, do not be surprised to see a more restrained, perhaps even humorous, Sugar on screen in the future. He has proved an unlikely television star, but a happy one.

'I never had any desire for fame or TV stardom, but I've enjoyed discovering the world of making television. When we made the first series of *The Apprentice* for

BBC2 in 2004/5, we had no idea how popular it would be or how long it would run. I thought it would just be a one-off. It has been a great experience.'

The Apprentice will see changes in future editions. The 2010 series will feature a number of of them, including the absence of Mountford. When she stepped away from *The Apprentice* fray, her replacement was Karren Brady. Sometimes dubbed 'football's first lady' (she was CEO of Birmingham City for years and is now vice chairman of West Ham United), Brady is one of Britain's leading businesswomen. 'She has a long track record in business and, because of football, Alan has worked with her,' Mountford said of the woman who will replace her at Sugar's side. 'They have a genuine connection.'

Brady was delighted with her new role. 'I am thrilled to be involved, having worked with Alan for 16 years,' she said. 'It's great to extend our relationship to the programme.' It has been a long and fruitful association. She even appeared on his shows, first as a contestant on *Comic Relief Does The Apprentice* in March 2007. There she was the leader of the ladies team and took them to victory, raising £776,000 for charity in the process. The following year she was appointed to the interview panel for the penultimate edition of *The Apprentice*, when Sugar's men and women grill the contestants fearsomely. She even offered a job to the runner-up for the 2008 series Claire Young.

Whether it is his family, employees or contacts, Sugar

has shown that loyalty is one of his key values. Given his riches, he has no material need to stand by those around him. He does so for the most sincere of reasons and thus finds himself in a virtuous circle, whereby the loyalty and love he offers to his family and friends returns to him on a regular basis. Think of all the multi-millionaires who have responded to their wealth by treating their staff with tyrannical disdain, who have dumped their wives for a gold-digging younger model, and who have disowned their family. Sugar could not be further from their example. Again, he benefits from his faithful ways too. While many wealthy men lead lives that are financially rich but emotionally poor, Sugar is a happy and contented man, surrounded by those who mean most to him and the emotion that means so much to him too – happiness.

Given that he has done a lot of his business overseas, there have sometimes been question marks over how much Lord Sugar loves his country. As we shall see, that love is deep and strong too.

CHAPTER FOUR
PATRIOTISM

Despite Samuel Johnson's belief that patriotism is 'the last refuge of the scoundrel', there is no doubt that it is one of the great British virtues. Down the years Great Britons have always been vocal and passionate in their love of their country. Lord Sugar is no different and for decades he has put his money where his mouth is by contributing enormously to the land he calls home, both through enormous taxation but also voluntary contributions of many different kinds.

However, to call Sugar patriotic is one of the less straightforward cases to make. After all, he became famed in the business world for his use of overseas manufacturing. During the early periods of his business Sugar routinely used Far East manufacturers because of the cheap prices such a route offered. To dismiss him as less than patriotic for making this choice, however, would be foolhardy. In using the Far East route he was merely ensuring the survival of his own fledgling *British* company and ensuring he could offer affordable prices to his *British* consumers.

Prior to this he had used patriotic imagery to help promote his products. Throughout the 1970s Amstrad produced advertisements that promoted the very Britishness of their products. The words 'British-made' would be prominently displayed as a logo, with a Union Jack wrapped round it. This was a common theme for advertisements during that decade, when a patriotic fervour swept the industry. Sugar was proud to be providing British products for British people and from a headquarters in the country's capital city. As he remembered of those days: 'We prided ourselves on being British manufacturers. And we used to buy components from Plessey, Mullard, IT&T – all the main British suppliers.'

It was only when he noticed that the components that he bought from these UK suppliers were actually made in Japan that Sugar changed his mind. Why, he wondered, was he buying from these domestic suppliers when he could just as easily go direct to the Japanese suppliers and – in cutting out the middle man – make savings that he could then pass on to the customer in the form of lower prices?

Therefore, during the 1980s he did a lot of business with Far Eastern suppliers, which led to doubts in some corners about patriotism. However, he was simultaneously becoming increasingly recognised as one of Britain's finest businessmen. As early as 1984 he was named the *Guardian* Young Businessman of the Year. His contribution to the British economy could not be denied. As David Thomas discovered in the 1980s, Sugar had contributed much to the British economy and was proud of doing so. Hanging on his office wall at Amstrad were reproductions of two cheques made out to the Inland Revenue: one for £25 million and one for £48 million. How many – if any – of Sugar's critics can point to anywhere near such a contribution to the British economy? And he has contributed many times more than that since.

'Manufacturing wealth is not the be-all and end-all of life,' said Lord Young in Sugar's defence. 'It's wealth creation that counts. That's sometimes done by manufacturing and sometimes done by service sector and other activities. Alan Sugar has enabled the British people to buy goods at better value than they would have otherwise. The more his computers are spread widely, the more they create wealth.'

Also, as author David Thomas pointed out, had Sugar not done so much manufacturing overseas then Amstrad could not have survived. The prices for the components needed were simply unreachable for him during the 1970s and 1980s. Indeed, by the end of the latter decade many other respected British companies had followed suit and taken their manufacturing east. He had blazed a trail for others and they were following keenly.

The second half of the 1980s saw another way in

which Sugar was, by trading with the Far East, boosting the cause of future British businessmen. The European Commission started to put 'anti-dumping' duties on electrical goods imported from Japan. Their motivation was to protect the European companies. However, some argued that it was a step that would ultimately harm those it was seeking to protect. Ultimately, they said, the economies of Europe would be harmed if low-price products were kept out.

Sugar was among those appalled by the 'anti-dumping' trend. It was not lost on him that huge European corporations such as Philips were very vocal in the lobbying. It was all very well for them, he felt, to be so agitated about low-cost Japanese products when they threatened the company's pre-eminent position. Philips could continue to sit pretty at the top of the tree and prices for the consumer would remain high as a result. However, it would not only be the punters who suffered, it would also see future Alan Sugars put at a disadvantage because they would be forced either to buy at inflated prices from European suppliers or build their own domestic factories. The latter was a particularly uninviting path: 'There's no such thing as a small chip plant or a small TV tube plant,' he explained. 'It's either £300 million or nothing.'

In 1986 he spoke out against the 'anti-dumping' trend, but admitted that his hands were tied in how much time and effort he could put into it. 'The legislation designed to protect European industry is actually having the reverse effect. But I'm too busy running the business and I have not the time, energy, patience or bureaucratic ways to fight the gnomes of Brussels.'

The following year the screw tightened on Amstrad as a result of the legislation, forcing him to take a more active role in the campaign. He had meetings with Government ministers, including the Trade and Industry Secretary Lord Young. As the minister told David Thomas, 'I had two or three meetings with him in the Department. And I had tremendous sympathy with him. I did all I could – he may not have thought I did – to help him through those problems. He had – and I know the type because I've been exactly the same way – no damn patience with all the officials, particularly in Brussels. But as a result of his case, I hope we're leaning more and more on Brussels.' The Government's ear might have been sympathetic, but its hands were largely tied too and it had to follow the European Commission's strictures.

Sugar went to the heart of the matter, flying to Brussels and speaking directly with those making these rules. Characteristically tough and uncompromising, he said that the commissioners were behaving as if they were an unpaid marketing department for large companies such as Philips and Thomson. He reflected on his way home that their policies were 'a total sham'. Speaking to the BBC he urged Prime Minister Margaret Thatcher to act. 'If she knew what was going on she would do her nut,' he said.

When he came to making satellite dishes for the launch of Sky TV, Sugar was clear that he wanted to match Rupert Murdoch's vision of 'a dawn of an age of freedom for viewing for ... the British public' by using British manufacturers to build the dishes. He believed the launch would benefit the nation on many levels: new choice in viewing, new prosperity for the economy and new jobs for British workers. He was also clear that he was aiming to – as he has so often in his career – bring lower prices to the public.

'It is our intention to manufacture these dishes and assemble the units in the UK,' he said at the launch. 'It would be very nice if we could manufacture them in an area of high unemployment. It is our intention to put our manufacturing process in that direction. At the moment, satellite television dishes on the UK market are selling for more than £1,000 and consumers are being asked to pay up to £200 for aerial erection. Those days are fast coming to an end. Our 60-centimetre dish, no bigger than an opened umbrella, does not need planning consent and will be erected by television aerial contractors for £40 or so.'

He then turned to the man next to him and lavished him with praise, as well as developing further his own patriotic theme. 'We are pleased that Rupert Murdoch has taken the initiative on this front. He has a reputation of getting things done and his proposal ... is very exciting.'

He was asked how their project for dishes was progressing. 'We are starting to tool-up for dishes and receivers,' he replied. 'Deliveries will start in the first quarter of 1989 at the rate of about 100,000 per month. We hope to set up a subcontractor in a high unemployment area for UK assembly.'

Sugar used the British firm General Electric Company (GEC) to make the dishes. He had worked with the managing director Lord Weinstock before and it proved to be an edge-of-your-seat affair in doing the deal for the satellite dishes. At one point, the entire deal seemed in jeopardy so he went directly to Weinstock to put him straight. 'I told him what was going on and that GEC was about to lose the order,' he explained. They tied up the details and the deal was struck. 'He liked doing the deal,' says Sugar. 'It reminded him of his early days, because him and me were haggling on the phone over 50 pence, which is probably something he hasn't done for 30 years.'

Although Sugar has a patriotic heart, he has a sensible business head, which had made him wary of doing business with British manufacturers. The GEC dishes deal, however, made him more receptive to the idea of doing such business domestically. He was particularly pleased with how fast GEC had worked. 'I must give them credit where credit's due,' he said. 'It brought back a lot of my confidence in British electronics when I saw them do that.'

Before long he had moved more of Amstrad's manufacturing to Britain. In 1999, he brought production of nearly a fifth of its PC2000 computer to a plant in Scotland. The plant was owned by his dish-manufacturers GEC. Significantly, the fact that Sugar moved production there saved 700 British jobs. Sugar was thrilled to pull that off and the sums worked for him too. He had done his calculations and worked out that even though it cost him an extra £10 to make these products in the UK, the flexibility it allowed him in terms of reacting quickly to market trends more than made up for that.

So it was that later that year he brought even more of his operation 'home'. Sugar gave the role of producing the new Amstrad fax machines to a factory in Northern Ireland, again boosting the British economy as his business mind became more comfortable with allying itself with his patriotic heart. Indeed, this meant that around a quarter of Amstrad products were now made in Europe, rather than the Far East. He predicted that this proportion of domestic production would increase in time. 'The Far East has no advantage any more in computers because in the past the most labour-intensive part was the building and testing of the main printed circuit board. Now, with automation and modern surface-mount technology, that does not require so much labour.'

Sugar was just as keen on domestic production when it came to his time in football. True, he brought some foreign players to the Premier League, notably the star German striker Jurgen Klinsmann, a signing that helped spark a stampede of foreign players into British football clubs. Never again would the top level of the British game be contested by clubs with mostly British players. However, again this can be viewed two ways. Some would say that the importing of so much foreign talent has harmed the British game. Others would say that Sugar was at the forefront of a trend to save a game which had lost much of its popularity and turned the Premiership into the most exciting and therefore commercial leagues on the planet.

Sugar has encouraged British football to remain true to its working-class roots. 'My concern is that the customers are the ones who will have to pay,' he said of the rising wage bills in the second half of the 1990s. 'I am not saying I am proud of this, but at Tottenham it must cost a man and two kids around £60 to £70 to watch a game. When I think back to my first job at the age of 17, I had a take-home wage of £11 a week. Then, it would have been inconceivable that one day it would cost £70 for a dad to take his two kids to a game. The danger is, if you extend the graph, that at the current rate it will eventually cost that bloke and his two kids £1,500!'

He also urged the clubs of Britain not to follow the poor example set by their high-spending equivalents in other European countries. 'The reality for the game is that it has to get worse before it will get better. There are irrational clubs around, not just in this country, but in places like Italy.'

He related a conversation he'd had with then Chelsea

FC supremo Ken Bates. 'He said, "We cannot cap players' wages." So he suggested that the Premier League and FA can cap the total wage bill of all the clubs. But that won't stop one club paying a fortune for Carlos Kick-a-Ball and give him £10 million a year, even if that meant sharing £2 million between the rest of the team.' His predictions were full of gloom. 'Of course, some irrational club will pay all this money, win the championship and there will be euphoria all round. What happens when this dies down? Reality hits them in the face and they'll have to pay off all the debts. I can see it clearly. Clubs will pay the money, whatever it is. But one day they will have to pay the price.'

Sugar has long spoken out in defence of the English league and with caution about the apparent march to a European super-league. 'As time goes by we're all going to consider ourselves Europeans, so it's not inconceivable that our weekly fixtures could be Manchester United flying off to play Juventus,' said Sugar in 2002. 'I foresee that's the only way it's going to go, which means that the Premier League will be a kind of upmarket Football League and the only way into this European League is to win that from time to time. At the moment most of the clubs in the Premier League are turning out to be cannon fodder for a nucleus of four or five clubs to get their fixtures played.'

Paul Thomsen, writing in London's *Evening Standard* in 2002, celebrated Sugar's attitude. 'At the time [1995] his predictions were dismissed by football and media alike, including this paper,' wrote Thomsen. 'They were the rantings of a "Johnny-come-lately" who had only been in the game five minutes. And when success failed to materialise at Spurs, his sweeping criticisms of everybody else found even less favour. But his words now appear to be prophetic. Yesterday, the G14 group of Europe's top clubs put football on the road to its first salary cap. Although one should stop short of declaring Sugar a sage, the Carloses at Bradford City and Derby County have plunged their clubs into deep trouble and the prune juice effect is wreaking havoc across all leagues, leaving clubs like Leicester City on the verge of bankruptcy. There is the first £100,000-a-week player while others take wage cuts – notions that would have been dismissed as nonsense in the past.'

And as Sugar has pointed out, the situation at club level has an effect at national level. 'We wonder why we can't put out a good England team. The reason is the Premier League attracts all the imports – as I put it 15 years ago, the Carlos Kick-a-balls who have no interest in the UK club they play for. They are playing for themselves. This is stopping young English players getting a chance to enhance their skills and learn their trade in the teams that they really love and admire – teams they really did follow as a boy.'

He reprised the theme while assessing the takeover of Manchester City FC by Arab billionaire Dr Sulaiman Al

Fahim in 2008. Comparisons were being made between himself and Al Fahim, but Sugar was having none of it. 'Well, we've both got beards [but] his daddy has loads of oil reserves,' he said.

Sugar's indictment was far-ranging and in your face. He said of the latest wave of foreigners: 'With the odd exception seen mostly in past years, these days players are heartless, disloyal and greedy. They are given a chance to display their skills in clubs like Spurs but, realistically, they are putting themselves on display.' The results of all this are serious and grave, he believes. He urged the owners of the Premiership's smaller clubs to set an example to the bigger boys. 'Give the English players and kids a run out and challenge them to beat the billionaire brigade. This will generate a winning, giant-killer spirit,' he said. Many bemoan the state of the English game, but it is typical and reflective of Sugar's vision that he also makes positive suggestions.

One of the patriotic Sugar's proudest moments came in 1999, when he was named on the New Years' honours list. The boy from Hackney was about to become *Sir* Alan Sugar. 'I'm tickled pink,' he said.

He then explained that he felt the significance of this news went far beyond the personal. 'It is a great honour and a wonderful sign of the times that a man that started his life in a working class background should, through hard work and application, be honoured by his country. Young people should take this as a signal that in Britain today anything is possible if the will to succeed is strong enough.'

Even amid this celebration he remembered his roots. 'My only regret is that my mum and dad are no longer here to enjoy this moment,' he sighed. What a proud day it was, though, when he went to Buckingham Palace to receive his knighthood on 13 June 2000. He was permitted to take just three guests and chose his wife Ann, daughter Louise and son Daniel. 'The kids had to fight over it. But they managed to arrive at a peaceful arrangement.'

When Sir Alan was called to approach the Queen for his knighthood, the announcer said that the honour was being bestowed upon him for his work with computers and electronics. However, the Queen told him that everyone would actually know him as a result of his involvement in football. She said that football must be a 'a rather precarious business'.

He smiled knowingly and replied, 'Yes, it certainly is.'

Amid the pride and celebration, he put the honour into a wider perspective, hoping to encourage others. 'It was a great day, a wonderful occasion. I seem to have come a long way and that is a great, great feeling,' he said. 'It shows how someone can start from a humble background and go on to be very successful. It shows the country that anything is possible. These honours certainly help break down the class barriers.'

He was also supportive of the monarchy in his sentiments. 'They are something the whole world takes the mickey out of but actually they are fantastic and really should be kept,' he said. 'We must start to appreciate that and leave them alone.'

The knighthood is not the only honour that has been bestowed upon him. Twelve years earlier, in 1988, Sugar had been made an Honorary Doctor of Science by City University. He had been involved with the business school, including establishing the Amstrad Research Scholarship. Five years after his knighthood Brunel University awarded him an Honorary degree of Doctor of Science. 'I am delighted to accept this degree from a famous University that specialises in technology, a field that has been close to my heart all of my professional life,' he said. 'It is a great honour they felt my contribution to technology over the years has warranted this.'

Sugar has also waved the flag for Britain on *The Apprentice* and, thanks to the ability of candidates to muck things up, this has often produced comical results. In week six of Series Three, he set the candidates the task of buying and selling British produce at a farmers' market in France. Paul Callaghan, one of the team leaders, took the novel route of buying budget-price British cheese and trying to sell it to foodie French customers. Naturally his plan backfired and the team lost the task, making just £225 to their opponents' £410, leading to his firing. Patriotism can only stretch so far. IT'S NO WONDER THEY GET FIRED, ran the resultant headline in the *Daily Star*.

It was a task that truly got the country talking but

Makro – the food suppliers responsible for the cheese Callaghan bought – were not happy about the image their products had garnered from the programme. So much so that they felt the need to go to France to repeat the task. Their sales results were certainly more successful than Callaghan's team's. Makro cheese buyer Andy Walsh said: 'British cheeses are increasingly popular in France, with sales rising by 20 per cent year on year. We stock over 200 different types of cheese from big national brands to small independent suppliers, like Wyke Farm, a family-run business from Somerset. Where the contestants on *The Apprentice* failed is not with the quality of the product they were offering but by not realising that the key to selling to the French is to appeal to their taste buds. They don't care about packaging or brand names. What they want is to try the food and, once they've tried it, they invariably like it and will buy it.'

Sugar is also part of a noble tradition of British Jews who have contributed hugely to British society in several fields. Jews have been in Britain since the 11th century. Shamefully they were expelled in 1290, but they were to return in 1656. However, it was not until the late 1800s that full-scale Jewish immigration began. The scale of their contribution has far exceeded their number, and the number of great British Jews is enormous. These include leading philosophers Sir AJ Ayer and Sir Isaiah Berlin, and celebrated intellectuals from Jacob Bronowski to

Elias Canetti. Then there are respected historians like Sir Martin Gilbert, Winston Churchill's official biographer and the author of over 80 historical works. In the world of business he is joined by Michael Marks of the legendary Marks & Spencer chain. Then there are politicians like Sir Malcolm Rifkind, Michael Howard and David Miliband. The story is just as strong in the legal system: Anglo-Jewry has provided several Lord Chief Justices and among our finest barristers are numerous men and women of Jewish descent. Sugar stands in several of these camps, having contributed to business, football and now politics.

It was partly Sugar's patriotism that brought him and the Prime Minister together. He had been praising of Gordon Brown as, via the pages of *The Sun* in 2008, he launched a campaign for British people to back British small businesses to help haul the country out of the financial mess. He suggested, too, that Brown's vision was now being taken up overseas too. 'It seems the Prime Minister has been very smart, as yesterday the Americans announced an almost carbon copy of his plans,' wrote Sir Alan, brushing off the disappointment at his recent failure to buy a stake in Woolworths. 'However, with all that banking stuff sorted, we have to consider ongoing issues. We are not out of the woods yet.'

Showing the sort of simple but effective vision that would see him rewarded with a role in Brown's administration, he offered his own method to help get

Britain back on its feet. 'I would never have thought I would be dishing out compliments to the French, but there are some things I admire about them. Chief among them was that the French public made a patriotic effort to buy French.' He encouraged the British public to do exactly the same. Not that he was absolving the Government of responsibility. 'If we the public are going to do our bit to get Britain back on track, the Government have to look at themselves and see what they can do. We're all in this together.'

Federation of Small Businesses chairman John Wright, who would later be critical of Sir Alan, agreed with his campaign. He said: 'Small businesses are the lifeblood of the country's economy. These measures, if implemented, will ensure they survive and prosper.'

Sun readers reflected the warmth in which Sugar's words were received among the ordinary folk of Britain. 'I agree with Sir Alan and support British industry,' said one. 'I own a small recruitment business built from my bedroom over ten years. In the past year I've lost six of 15 staff. It is very hard.'

Another wrote to say: 'Sir Alan Sugar couldn't be more right. I found his article truthful, hard hitting and very supportive towards the British public. The Government should take a leaf out of his book.' Ever a man to chime with the tabloid-reading ordinary folk of Britain, this was another moment where Sugar's common touch hit the mark.

He has supported numerous such initiatives, not just that of *The Sun*. In January 2009 he fronted a *Daily Mirror* campaign that urged readers to 'Buy British'. He said: 'We must buy products that are made here ... supporting a British firm creates work for someone.'

Joined by Sir Richard Branson and Theo Paphitis in leading a chorus of support for the plan to help small firms, Sir Alan said: 'All small businesses have to start from somewhere and banks at the moment are not very receptive as they only want safe bets on big organisations. But if they continue in this cautious manner there will be no chance for small business to grow or survive.

'It's time to worry about ourselves and forget globalisation stuff for a while. Many foreign companies don't even pay taxes in the UK. So if anyone is thinking of buying stuff, try to hunt around to support a British firm as in our little way we're creating work for someone down the line ... The Government's latest initiative to provide funding for small- to medium-size business is an excellent idea: it's exactly what is needed in these tough times. If we have any chance of getting out of this financial crisis it will only happen if people are employed and earning money.'

The chief of the Prince's Trust, Martina Milburn, supported Sugar's words and felt they would help give encouragement and backing to entrepreneurs. 'But as the economic downturn gathers pace, the Alan Sugars of tomorrow may feel it is too risky to start up alone. Letting this entrepreneurial talent go to waste would be a disaster for the economy. The *Daily Mirror* is right to highlight the plight of small businesses.'

On television Sugar is a beacon of pride for the British people. Although *The Apprentice* originated in the US, the British version has since been sold over there. When American viewers got their first glimpse of the UK version of *The Apprentice*, they were curious to know, as one American newspaper put it, whether 'You're fired' sounds better in a British accent. The verdicts were mixed. The *Baltimore Sun* described the show as 'a guilty pleasure', the reviewer describing himself as 'an Anglophile' and stating that Sugar made Donald Trump 'seem like a wimp'. The reviewer was impressed by Sugar's genuine, straight-talking British style. 'As much as we hate the contestants, Alan Sugar seems to hate them far more.' Another US publication made a less flattering conclusion. When the Michigan newspaper the *Lansing State Journal* wrote up the British version of *The Apprentice*, it said: 'In this version, crusty Sir Alan Sugar does the hiring. Unlike the US version, this doesn't seem obsessed with telegenic contestants. Also, it rains a lot.'

Crusty or not, Sugar is a patriotic Brit and as such cares for our interests and represents our fair isle brilliantly, come rain or shine. No wonder he has inspired so many across Britain. What is perhaps less well celebrated, though, is his bounteous work for charitable causes. By any standards he has always been a generous man, one of life's givers. It is to that side of his life that we now turn.

CHAPTER FIVE
CHARITY AND INSPIRATION

Tales of Lord Sugar's generosity appear regularly throughout his life story, as we have already seen in the chapter on Family Values and Loyalty. If ever a person proved true the idea that if you share you ultimately end up richer, then he is that man. In his regular and far-reaching charity activities, in the way he treats his staff and also in his day-to-day life, Sugar is frequently extremely kind, unselfish and giving.

True, a handful of former employees have made harsh allegations against him but plenty more have spoken emotionally of the kindness he showed them. Just ask his long-term public relations ally and *Apprentice* sidekick Nick Hewer. When Hewer left Amstrad, Lord Sugar laid on a dinner at the Dorchester for him and 100 guests. 'Sir Alan is a very generous friend,' Hewer says. 'The best thing about working for him was there was always something going on. He has vibrancy about him.'

He does indeed and Sugar has not reached the heights of business power and wealth by treading on those who work for him. Throughout the history of Amstrad there are tales of him making decisions that involved sacrifice for him while his staff benefitted. A powerful illustration of this occurred in the mid-1980s. As the business world was increasingly considered to be an arena of greed, and some feared that the likes of Sugar were drowning in an ocean of self-centred 'me, me, me' culture, he took a decision that speaks volumes.

At the time, his company's profits were very much on the rise, thanks in the main to success in the computer market. Watching this trend, Sugar's financial advisers strongly encouraged him to further increase the level of the dividends paid out to Amstrad shareholders. If was a measure, he was assured, that would placate Amstrad's critics in the City. Sugar was having none of it, despite the fact that with a personal shareholding of nearly 50 per cent, he would have enjoyed a colossal payday had he followed their advice. He overlooked his own personal gain in order to protect the livelihoods of his employees.

This was not the only such incident in the 1980s. In 1985, Amstrad ran its first share option scheme for employees. Widespread in business, the schemes represent a good way of rewarding staff for hard work and motivate them to greater heights – everybody benefits. However, few other companies offered share options as widely as Amstrad. Employees around the world, from directors right down to the most junior staff, were included in the scheme. In total, 11.55 million shares were offered and the dividend three years later was to the value of around $500,000 each. It was a very generous structure for Sugar to use – and that generosity did not go unnoticed by the bean counters.

At the following annual general meeting of Amstrad, the institutional investors expressed their extreme disquiet at the level of generosity Sugar had shown with his share scheme. They encouraged him to rein it in, but Sugar stood by his move and vowed to continue offering his staff this route to personal fortune.

Make no mistake, though, Sugar could be a formidable employer. He has never been one to suffer fools gladly but it went further than that. 'You cannot work for Sugar unless you are of sound mind,' explained one man who passed through Amstrad. 'If you are one of these people who takes things personally, you will have no future with that company. You have to let it slip off your back.'

The same employee recalls that he had to resort to heart-to-hearts with his father in order to survive the baptism of fire he received from Sugar when he first joined Amstrad. 'The guy is out for me,' he told his father. 'He wants my blood for some reason. He scares me. There's no other word I can use but fear.'

His father called it right, identifying what was really

going on. 'Stick it out,' he told his son. 'He's trying to test you.' In time his father's words were richly vindicated.

Sugar's approach to the employee might have been tough, but it was tough love. When the same employee scored a major marketing triumph, prompting a glowing review of an Amstrad computer in an influential magazine, Sugar was plentiful and warm in his praise. He ran to the employee's desk holding the review. 'Have you done this? Is this your work? Are you responsible? This is bloody amazing!' He then went from desk to desk telling other staff of the man's triumph, even faxing the review to Amstrad outposts across the globe. From that day onwards, Sugar's tough approach to him was gone. He had earned his respect.

Those who might question Sugar's approach should listen to the words of the same man when asked to sum up his time working for Sugar. 'I love the guy,' he told David Thomas. 'I walked in there a smug young man of 22. And I had the crap knocked out of me for six months. I became a hard-nosed salesman and a professional. That was due to Alan Sugar. You go into the Alan Sugar school of management and you get the fat worked off you.' It was rough-and-ready but well thought out and, ultimately, a successful management strategy.

In that man's experiences we see another level of generosity in Sugar. Here he did not give up anything physical or immediately tangible. However, a major sacrifice was made. Sugar was willing to give up his popularity and good name to get the best out of an employee. He would have known full well that at first the employee would be telling people all manner of nasty stories about his treatment. Full of self-belief as ever, Sugar was willing to take this tough step in order to get the best out of his employee and in doing so allow him to reach the heights of his own abilities. The loving way that the man remembers Sugar and his time with him speaks volumes about how effectively and keenly this worked. Sugar often made the same sacrifice to help his staff and clients reach their full potential.

In 1984 the advertising agency Delaney Fletcher Delaney pitched for a contract to promote Amstrad's computers. Greg Delaney led the pitch and presented three different concepts to Sugar. The Amstrad boss was ruthlessly dismissive of the first, said the second one was OK and declared that the third one was closer to the mark. He then abruptly closed the meeting and walked out. Only those who worked closely with Sugar would know that this actually constituted a very positive response from him. He was rarely given to generous praise of people's work, because that would lead, he believed, to them becoming complacent and underachieving. Again, it was a tough but kind and effective technique from the man at the top. The generosity was hidden but indubitable – he was helping people get the best out of themselves with no regard to their short-term, or even long-term, perception of him.

Sugar doesn't simply put his money where his mouth is: he puts his time where his mouth is also. 'I personally believe you have to plough something back,' he says of the talks he has often given to young business students. 'It's the easiest thing in the world to write out a cheque and of course that just deals with your conscience. I feel I go beyond that by actually wanting to get involved at a grass roots level. I talk to young people about enterprise and try to share with them how I made it and how they might be able to make it. I go anywhere within reason once a month, because they are an audience willing to listen.' True, he often tests such audiences with his direct message, but still they queue up for an hour or two of Sugar wisdom. He does not deliver such speeches for the money, he does so because he wants to inspire those present.

He has also supported cultural activities which might surprise those who only know him in passing from occasional television viewings. Regular *Apprentice* viewers will know about his support for the Hackney Empire theatre, for instance, which he has featured in tasks on the show. He is now a patron of the plush, charming theatre. Built on Mare Street, Hackney in 1901, this Grade II listed building has seen such luminaries as Charlie Chaplin, WC Fields, Stan Laurel and Marie Lloyd perform in its hall.

Sugar regularly built *Apprentice* tasks around the theatre, bringing both attention and funds to this national institution. In Series One he set the candidates the challenge of negotiating with five celebrities and convincing the stars to donate their property or services to a charity auction in aid of the refurbishment of the theatre. One of the celebrities was Paul McKenna and candidate Raj, a fan of the hypnotist, chose to lead the negotiations. In the event, Raj was toe-curlingly star-struck and rambled embarrassingly at McKenna until fellow candidate Paul intervened and took over the lead. Meanwhile, eventual winner Tim managed to offend Arsenal footballer Ian Wright during their negotiations and had to be bailed out by Miriam. On the night of the auction, there was more toe-curling when the theatre tickets donated by comedian Mel Smith almost failed to sell.

In the end, Ben's Impact team won by raising £18,000 to their rivals' £10,000. Not only had the task raised funds for the Empire, it had also raised awareness of the venue, injecting all concerned with new confidence and vigour. This is something it is hard to put a price on.

In the mid-1980s, Sugar set up the Alan Sugar Foundation as a vehicle to donate money to other charities. During the first six years of its existence alone it was enormously generous, donating a total of £1,672,795 to a number of causes. Among these were the British Lung Foundation, the National Youth Theatre and the British Equestrian Olympic Fund. The Samaritans and the Great Ormond Street Hospital also benefitted, the latter to the tune of £150,000. The

Ravenswood Foundation, which cares for the mentally handicapped, were handed £157,000 and became a regular beneficiary of the Alan Sugar Foundation.

A number of Jewish causes also received donations, including the Jewish Blind Society, the Holocaust Educational Trust and Group Relations Educational Trust. Jews College, London was given £40,000. Some £5,000 was given to the Ashten Trust, a Jewish educational charity. But the cause that benefitted most from the Foundation in its opening years was Jewish Care, a charity that looks after the elderly, frail, sick and vulnerable across London and the south-east with an enormous range of services and activities. In 1994 he donated £1.1 million to an old people's home in Ilford to build a new extension, called the Sugar Wing in his honour.

Jewish Care is a prestigious charity that has drawn praise from some fine quarters. For instance, former Prime Minister Tony Blair told them, 'Jewish Care is not just Jewish values in action; it is actually the best of British values in action. You can be really, really proud of the work that you do.' Sir Alan can also be proud of the work that the Alan Sugar Foundation does.

Perhaps it is this side of Sugar that was so appalled by the ways of the football community during his tempestuous years in the game. He described the players as 'transient mercenaries', their ways all too often at odds with his. *Scotland on Sunday* magazine profiled Sugar in 1997 and summed up the warm heart he keeps hidden under his at times cold exterior. It described him as a member of 'a rather cautious and honourable breed underneath the verbals'. All the same, as the press pointed out in the wake of Sugar's outburst, many footballers are generous donors to charity, and some even have their own charities. This trend is a relatively recent one to gather pace, however. Sugar's assessment of footballers may well be a generalisation but that does not mean it comes without merit. He does not see football and charity as exclusive spheres. Indeed, when Sugar fell out with his star signing at White Hart Lane, striker Jurgen Klinsmann, he gave a famous television interview after the German left Tottenham Hotspur, in which he suggested that the reporter sell Klinsmann's replica shirt and donate the proceeds to a charitable cause.

'Look what he's written on there – "To Alan with a very special thank you,"' he said, brandishing the shirt. 'I'm bloody sure it's very special because I'm the bloomin' mug who re-launched his career. I wouldn't wash my car with this shirt now. You can give it to one of your viewers if you like or auction it and give the money to some charity. Obviously an appropriate charity if we can. Something like a charity to get people to tell the truth in future or something like that.' His words might have seemed humorous but it was in keeping with his approach to charity that he should spot, if only jokingly, such an opportunity.

Sugar is an inspirational man who sets an example. To

his personal delight, his television shows have motivated many to embark on charitable ventures. In 2007, when the Sheffield Children's Hospital Charity went on the hunt for a new fundraiser to join its team, they decided to conduct the search along the lines of Sugar's hit television show, *The Apprentice*. David Vernon-Edwards, director of the charity, explained: 'We've launched our own *Apprentice*-style scheme to try to encourage a wide range of people to apply for the position.'

The same happened further north in England the following year when the Stockton charity A Way Out also chose to model its quest for a new fundraiser on the programme's example. 'We do not expect it to be the interview from hell but it will be challenging,' said a spokesperson, paraphrasing Sugar's famous boast that the show is 'an interview from hell'. Oz Experience, a project organised by the Joshua Foundation charity, also ran an *Apprentice*-themed event in Manchester to raise money for its cause.

In November 2009, a grand venue in Aberdeen was the site for the celebration of yet another charitable function inspired by Lord Sugar. Proof that he continually helps to put the Great back into Britain came when an *Apprentice*-style task raised £140,000 for a local cancer charity called Clan (Cancer Link Aberdeen and North). The Urquhart Partnership and the Acumen Group, who organised the 'UPprentice' scheme, handed 15 teams £100 and challenged them to make as much money as possible for charity in just six weeks. The ideas were plentiful and varied, ranging from a sponsored superhero walk to work to producing recipe books and shining shoes.

Urquhart Partnership MD Campbell Urquhart beamed: 'Those who participated in the UPprentice have shown an enormous amount of commitment to the challenge, and their creativity and business acumen has helped to raise thousands for a very worthwhile cause.' Lord Sugar would have heartily approved. In a separate move in the same year he joined other celebrities in donating his handprint to be auctioned off for charity.

Viewers of *The Apprentice* will probably remember the 'Pantsman' character created by contestant Philip Taylor in the 2009 series of the hit show. In episode five, Sugar set them the task of coming up with a concept to advertise a breakfast cereal brand. Taylor's concept was to call the cereal 'Pantsman' to tie it in with the early morning process of getting dressed. He even created a 'Pantsman' dance which was compared to the excruciating moves of David Brent in the television comedy *The Office*. Taylor's fellow contestant Kimberly Davies told him: 'I think that's verging on being silly now.' 'Pantsman' became the talk of the nation's viewers the day after the show, but it had a serious legacy too.

In July 2009 Taylor helped promote the Everyman charity, which raises awareness of male cancer. Thanks to his 'Pantsman' image, Taylor was considered the man to help encourage men to take the threat of testicular cancer seriously. Taylor also took part in 2009's Great North Run to raise money for the Water Aid charity. To help raise media coverage of the race, he agreed to dress up as 'Pantsman' for the run. 'We can all take clean water for granted but sadly that is not the case for more than two billion people in the world. That's a great reason to put "Pantsman" into action,' he said.

Taylor is not alone in using his *Apprentice*-earned profile to help the needy. The original winner of *The Apprentice* has used his experience to do charitable work. Tim Campbell, the man who was crowned as Sugar's first apprentice, launched a charitable concern in November 2008 with the assistance and backing of London mayor Boris Johnson. The Bright Ideas Trust will fund and support entrepreneurship in deprived areas of inner city London, targeting 16- to 30-year-olds who want to set up their own businesses. The first areas targeted by the charity were the Olympic boroughs of Greenwich, Hackney, Newham, Tower Hamlets and Waltham Forest in east London, but it plans to move far beyond these.

'To be successful, it is important to be focused,' said Campbell. 'We're not social workers or psychiatrists. But if you want to start a business, we aim to give all the help you need to get that off the ground.' When asked by the *Financial Times* which single individual had been most influential on his own career, he named Lord Sugar: 'An awesome person to have worked with. He gave me the confidence to start my own business and become self-motivated. His input ultimately led to me setting up the Bright Ideas Trust.'

So there we have Sugar's generous nature encouraging someone who uses that motivation to do charitable work – a virtuous circle indeed. Sugar is famous for installing confidence in his *Apprentice* winners. When he told the winner of the 2009 series, Yasmina Siadatan, how he regarded her, he drew on his own early experiences to fill her up with motivation and self-belief.

'Yasmina, I think of myself at your age,' he told her. 'I was nine years younger than you when I started my business. Two years later, I could honestly say I was made. I didn't have loads of money but what I did know was I didn't need anybody else. I could do it myself. And I think you could do it yourself. You've done it.' She was pleased with his words, and her response showed how they had connected with and motivated her. 'I'm damn good at what I do, I've got a spark about me and I'm a risk-taker,' she beamed. 'I've got something different about me.'

The same month as Lord Sugar took his place in the House of Lords, his role as a leader and motivator was made clear. He inspired a group of Leeds College of Technology students to open their own clothing company, Nexus Clothing. Following the Sugar way, they set up a rough-and-ready stall in the college during busy periods of the day and flogged their clothing to fellow students. The chairman confirmed that they had been inspired by Sugar's example. 'We are expecting our sales to escalate once the word gets out and people start wearing the clothes to college. It's a really exciting venture for all of us,' he said. 'We all watch *The Apprentice* and have been inspired to really push this project and earn some money.'

Sugar's influence spans generations, too. Anthony Vazquez-Phillips of Croydon has been named 'the next Alan Sugar' at the tender age of just 16. 'I made my first sale when I was ten years old: the inside of a toilet roll wrapped in wrapping paper as a cracker,' he said. 'Although it was for school and I didn't get to keep the money it was brilliant.' Since that unlikely starting point his fortunes have soared. 'Now I am managing director of the company at school and have my own company and am involved in the marketing with other projects. I could sell anything,' he said. Sugar was told by his headmaster that he could sell anything, too.

The similarities do not end there, for Anthony, like Sugar, has taken his business skills and used them to charitable effect. 'At school I became involved in a company which gets clothes from a charity in Bangalore. We sell the clothes and then send the profits back. It is important to do something for charity.'

It's all a glorious response for a boy who has been bullied at school. As to the future, he has firm ambitions – one of which might see him cross Lord Sugar's path. He said: 'I want to prove to everyone that I can do it. You never know, I might have a great idea and be on *Dragons' Den* or *The Apprentice*. That would show those bullies.'

These are no flash-in-the-pan examples of the Sugar effect. Teenagers are showing an increasing interest in aptitude for business. With television shows such as *Dragons' Den*, *The Apprentice* and *Tycoon* making business sexy, the increase in entrepreneurial spirit among the young is rocketing. In May 2009 a group of teenagers were asked to prove their business acumen in a novel enterprise. Make Your Mark With A Tenner sent youngsters out into the world with just £10 and encouraged them to make a profit. It was a scheme influenced by Lord Sugar's tasks on *The Apprentice* and garnered results that were interesting and varied, and bode well for the future of the British economy. More than that, it also brought happy headlines about the UK's teens in a time when concerns about truancy, drug-use and knife crime have all too often painted a depressing portrait of our young.

Another young man following in Sugar's footsteps is 20-year-old Fraser Doherty. After deciding to turn his childhood jam-making hobby into a business, he created a range called SuperJam. His products are now stocked in over 1,000 British supermarkets and his company is expected to sell over a million pounds' worth of jam in 2010. But Doherty also decided to share the fruits of his success charitably after being taken on a life-changing visit by his grandmother to lonely old people's homes. He recalled: 'I remember some of the people crying when we left. Ever since I have wanted to help where I can.' He began to arrange and host SuperJam Tea Parties to bring isolated pensioners together for some jam, music and a chat. There have been over 100 parties so far. The beneficiaries of the events are widespread: the assembled oldies knit tea-cosies and blankets, which Doherty sends to Indian orphans.

Sugar is pleased to have inspired these young men, but is keen to emphasise that real life is the best example to learn from, rather than the printed page. 'I've never been a great believer in [business self-help books],' he said. 'I am a firm believer that if you've got what it takes, you'll have a feeling in your gut, a hunger in your belly – and you'll know you want to be your own boss.' He later added: 'You can't learn to be an entrepreneur by reading a book. You can only find out by giving it a try. Don't worry if you make mistakes, because that's how most people learn.'

Sugar respects those who make their way in business, just as he deeply admires those who use their riches to benefit good causes. Many of his friends and associates have done just that and he is always quick to praise them for it. When he attended the funeral of his friend, the television entertainer Jeremy Beadle in 2008, he was at pains to emphasise his generosity. 'Jeremy was one of the most generous people I have ever come across. He did so much work behind the scenes for many great causes,' he said. It was all true: Beadle raised over £100 million for charities in his life.

Sugar's long-time ally Margaret Mountford is another generous and charitable character. For instance, in 2009 she became the public face of the legacy consortium Remember a Charity. A trustee of the heart-disease charity Corda, Mountford encouraged her fellow lawyers to remind people of the option to leave money in their wills to good causes. 'As a retired lawyer, I recognise that will-writing professionals could play an important role in changing the status quo,' said Mountford. She has also undertaken much more charitable work, including being a guest speaker at an event for an African charity based in Ulster. 'I was lucky because I was good at school and fell into the right career at the right time. And in that respect I should give something back,' she said.

Sugar commands high sums for his services in speeches, appearances and writings. Almost invariably, though, he passes on the full fee he receives to charities, including his fee for *The Apprentice*. The same is true of his many articles. For instance, the fee for his popular Spoonful of Sugar business advice column in the *Daily Mirror* in the 1990s went to charities supporting youth employment and enterprise. How did the shy man from Hackney come to command such fees? How did he become such an entertaining character? We shall find out in the coming pages...

CHAPTER SIX
ENTERTAINMENT

The opening titles played of *The Apprentice* are played out to its theme tune, Prokofiev's *Dance of the Knight*. Dru Masters, the musical director of the series, explained how they came by this choice. 'We decided early on that, musically, the programme would have a slightly '60s, '70s caper movie feel, sort of *The Italian Job* meets *Ocean's Eleven*,' he said. 'We had no music for the opening titles. They were thinking of running some kind of M People-style "inspirational" pop song, which I thought would have been disastrous. So I played them the Prokofiev march out of desperation. And suddenly it was like it had always been there. It provides this suitably bombastic backdrop for Sir Alan to ham it up.' And ham it up he does.

Anyone who has tuned in to *The Apprentice* can see that Sugar is entertaining. Strangely for a man who has often been shy – painfully so in his youth – he has become a television star. From the first series he proved to have a knack for a witty putdown. Those who had followed his career closely will not have been surprised by his way with words. His statements as Amstrad chairman had often been amusing affairs: he once described a rival company as behaving 'like a lost lamb with a shopping basket'.

Everybody has their own favourite *Apprentice* quip. One of the earliest standout moments came when Series One candidate Paul Torrisi was being grilled during a boardroom exchange. 'I am a Roman Catholic,' said Torrisi, 'and as God is my witness, I shook her hand outside.'

Sugar's quick-fire response?

'Yeah? Well, I'm Jewish and I couldn't care less.'

Sugar's entertaining words of warning to the contestants quickly became a highlight of the show. He could scarcely stop daring them to underestimate him at their peril. On occasion during his fog-horn alerts he stumbled upon the territory of malapropisms too. 'You are not here to enhance some form of media career,' he told contestants, 'so if any of you gentlemen are thinking of prancing around in your Calvin Kleins, showing off your three-piece-suite bulge you can forget about it.'

Sometimes the contestants would bite back – or try to. When one questioned the fairness of the contest, Sugar gave them short shrift. '*Fair*? The only fair you're gonna get is your bloody train fare home.' Another word of warning was even more to the point: 'If you survive here, I promise you this: as sure as I've got a hole in my bloody a**e, when it's down to two of you people that are nice about you *now* ... will not be.'

The viewers lapped all this up. The more uncomfortable the atmosphere in the boardroom for the candidates, the more amused and gripped they were back home. It was certainly uncomfortable for Tuan Le when Sugar told him: 'You couldn't close a barn door even if you tripped over it!' Le's shy demeanour made him one of those candidates just tailor-made for a dressing down from Sugar.

Others, though, perplexed him and seemingly unsettled him a bit. Jo Cameron was one such person. Eccentric and a bit dotty, she unsettled Sugar, who told her at one point: 'I just don't know whether you're some sort of bloody nutter.' He also once said of her: 'It says here she used to train Financial Directors for MG Rover. No wonder they went bloody skint!'

On occasion his exasperation was immense, such as during one week of Series Two when he threatened to bend the rules and do a mass firing, such was his disappointment at their performance. 'I have got to fire someone, although quite frankly I'd like to get rid of the bleeding three of you,' he told them, prompting gulps of anxiety across the panel.

The Apprentice boardroom was no place for the faint-hearted, much to the amusement of viewers watching from the comfort of their sofas. In Series Three he turned on hapless Rory, sparing him no blushes at all. 'You're a disaster, an absolute disaster. I've given you the chance to explain yourself and you haven't. I was told that you were bankrupt; there's no shame in that, been bankrupt twice. Well, here's the hat-trick … Rory, you're fired!'

Sugar took a similarly direct route in dismissing Nicholas in the following series. 'You were devastated when you got a B in your GCSE French,' he reminded him of a remark on his CV. 'You're going to be even more devastated now, because you've got a big "F". You're fired!'

After the infamous selling-cheese-in-France task, he dispatched Paul, the losing team leader, hilariously. 'I sent you to sell the best of British to France. You spent half the bloody day frying sausages on some stupid contraption that the Boy Scouts could have made, and worse than that, Paul, you went out and lost me money! You're a total shambles. You're fired!'

He told Mani Sandher: 'As times have changed, you seem to have gone from anchor to w****r.' Ouch.

To Syed Ahmed he was scarcely more kindly: 'I've heard you managed the Titanic restaurant. Well, this is another disaster…'

His entertaining side was not one-dimensional, however. Where he felt it appropriate he would list the positive attributes of a candidate, while still firing them from the show. 'Simon, if I asked you to build me a wall, you'd build me a wall, I'm pretty sure of that. If I asked you to dig me a trench, you'd dig me a trench. But I'm not sure that if I asked you to run my investment portfolio, you'd be able to do that very well. I'm sorry, my friend, I think you're a little bit out of your depth here. And with regret, you're fired.'

Indeed, the candidates were often not upset with but appreciative of Sugar's honesty. 'I come from a world where everything is politically correct,' said Series One winner Tim Campbell. 'Being in a situation where things are actually expressed was quite refreshing. It may seem brutal, but for me it was always fair.'

Sometimes, however, it was beyond the kindest of people to be kind to a candidate. Take Michael Sophocles, who managed to mangle up the Muslim and Jewish faiths during a task in Morocco – despite claiming to be Jewish himself. Sugar was fuming and disgusted. He told the candidate: 'It's an insult to the Muslim religion, let alone the Jewish religion. On your CV, what did you say on there? You're a good Jewish boy...'

Sophocles was on the ropes, and replied: 'I'm not, I'm only half Jewish, Sir Alan.'

This is not possible, as according to Jewish law one is only Jewish if one's mother is Jewish (or if one has converted). So Sugar repeated the question: 'Well, you either are or you aren't, yeah? OK, because if you're unsure, you can always pull down your trousers and we can check.' The other candidates – and a nation watching at home – cracked up in amusement at Sugar's words and Sophocles's discomfort.

In Series Five he was back to issuing memorable warnings to the contestants. 'You think you can play and second guess me?' he asked them. 'Well, let me tell you – I am as hard to play as a Stradivarius. And you lot, I can tell you, are as easy to play as bongo drums!'

This was not him playing up for the cameras – Sugar could be just as outspoken and dramatic in real-life meetings in real-life boardrooms. Someone who sat in on a meeting between Sugar and Dixons said, 'These were not meetings where you would want to talk unless you had to, because you would get ripped apart – by your own side if not the other. They were fighting over volume and percentage points for hours and hours.' The air would turn blue, desks would be thumped.

However, says the same eyewitness, after slagging each other off throughout the meeting, Sugar and the Dixons people would then step outside the meeting room and laugh about the whole thing. This ability to separate the rough and tumble of the meeting room and the outside world has been key to Sugar's business progress. Indeed, much as he is proud of his more direct on-screen boardroom moments, he is keen to stress that there is more to him than the grump-bag that is all too often broadcast.

'What you see on screen is me, there's no question of that,' said Sugar. 'But it is the side of me the BBC chooses to show. There is more light-hearted banter, which hits the cutting-room floor because it doesn't put bums on seats. It's a one-way portrayal, not the whole of me.'

In the early days of Amstrad, his style of speaking was one that his underlings noted. Some of them attempted to copy it, but they often missed the subtleties of the Sugar way. 'They imitated his aggressiveness, the worst side of his character, without having the intelligence to know that beneath it was a very perceptive, humorous, intelligent guy,' said a retail associate of Sugar. Another Amstrad insider also detected a difference between Sugar and his impersonators: when Sugar told customers to 'bugger off', he did so with a twinkle in his eye. For Sugar the real world is just as much of a stage as his television appearances.

The early years of the 21st century had seen a glut of reality television shows before *The Apprentice* arrived and the critics were always on the lookout for a flop they could sharpen their pens on. With Sugar hardly the most loved or telegenic of men, there seemed here to be the prospect of a show that would face a critical panning. However, as all involved in the series were winners, it proved to be very, very successful. The viewer ratings were impressive, at first averaging around 2.5 million but climbing to around 4 million viewers by the end of the series.

The critical reception was also pleasing for all involved. *The Sun* said it was, 'the thinking man's reality show', while *The Mirror* described it as 'jaw-dropping viewing'. Broadsheet newspapers were head-over-heels too, with *The Daily Telegraph* calling it 'the most addictive show in years' and the *Guardian* saying that it provided 'a salutary lesson in aggressive buying and selling, hiring and firing'. *The Sunday Times* said that it was 'not just a game show: it's a business school'. Maverick editor-writer-publisher James Brown, writing in the *Independent* gushed, 'There is a feeling among reality-TV experts that *The Apprentice* may be the best programme of its genre ever shown on British television. It has all the trappings of core reality programming, a group of ordinary people who want something and are tested on television to get it.'

One response deserves to be quoted more fully. Journalist Leo McKinstry penned a heart-pumping tribute to the show in the *Daily Mail*. 'Indeed, *The Apprentice* runs against the fashionable values, not just of the BBC, but of our entire society. In our culture of grievance, with its shrill emphasis on employee rights, it is wonderfully refreshing to have a programme that does not treat its participants as victims and does not regard pressure as a dirty word. In a world of compensation and industrial tribunals, where it is virtually impossible to sack any public employee, no matter how incompetent, it is a pleasant shock to hear failure met with the phrase: "You're fired!" Those words contain a beautiful, unemotional purity. At least in *The Apprentice*, if not in Labour's Britain – or more specifically, in Tony Blair's Government – individuals are held to account for their performances.'

Brown then turned to the star of the show, writing: 'Then it has its honey-trap character, a magnetic personality who emerges during the series and stealthily gets you obsessed. This person, naturally, is Sugar: a rough-and-ready, straight-talking, self-made East End trader, manufacturer and landlord who has honed his instinct for a deal into a billion-dollar business. On top of this, the programme-makers have shot London from the air in the style of Hollywood legends Michael Mann and David Fincher, and added a soundtrack that ratchets up the tension.'

The first series won a host of awards, including the Most Popular Reality Show at the 2005 National Television Awards. Sugar has since said that he had foreseen all this popularity. He explained that on starting work on it, he quickly realised just how exciting and successful the show was going to be. Asked if he expected it to become a hit, he said: 'Yes, I did actually. Not when they first asked me, but when I could see how it was going from the slices I was shown by the production crew. What you see is me, there's no acting, and the same goes for the apprentices. It has been an amazing experience, in that I've learnt about the world of television and how to make a TV programme. Hats off to the production team, because for every one of those episodes, there must have been 35 hours of film. They've had to watch it all and edit it down. The BBC have spent money on quality. Then again, they'll be able to use those opening shots again in a second series. Would I do a second series? Yes.'

However, on the question of scheduling, he was somewhat more critical. 'If I have any criticism of the BBC, it is only that they picked a poor night by scheduling it on Wednesday, because it clashes with the Champions League. The first few weeks they were ecstatic, because they were attracting the elusive audience of 29- to 35-year-old boyos, the yuppies, the upwardly-mobile aspiring boyos. But then these guys also have Sky Plus, so I think we're losing a lot of the audience figures to people who are watching it an hour later, after the football.' He then moved closer to home to underline his point. 'I can give you no better example than my own two sons. Last week they watched Chelsea-Arsenal first on Sky and then their dad afterwards on Sky Plus.' He added with a grin: 'That's loyalty for you.'

However, overall Sugar was very much enjoying the show and happy with how it turned out. 'It's 80 per cent business and 20 per cent fun,' he told one interviewer. 'If you saw the American one – which I thought was crap – and then you see with ours that there's less glitz and showbiz here. You can follow what's going on. The American one – the business side – was very hard to follow.'

Not all who have crossed paths with Sugar and *The Apprentice* are quite as positive about the experience. All the same, they cannot deny that the show provides top entertainment for the viewers. *The Apprentice* editor Dan

Adamson maintains that the editing is fair and that 'Sir Alan especially' would never let it become a sexed-up reality show. However one ousted contestant, Sharon McAllister, says, 'It's bull**** to describe it as a business programme. It's entertainment. Everything is edited according to Sir Alan's final decision. I was made out to be a whinger and I'm not.'

Badger was more amusing about her surprise on watching the edited programmes. 'Watching it afterwards, there were loads of things I cringed about. Why I look like a bulldog chewing a wasp for the first three weeks I have no idea. And the stupid outfits they made you wear – my life!'

Sugar has proved an entertaining guest on television chat shows, a raconteur even. On one of his appearances on *Friday Night With Jonathan Ross*, he rolled out an amusing tale of a toilet malfunction that took place during a visit to a restaurant. 'I was standing there trying to do my stuff and this bloke is next to me going, "Cor, that geezer was horrible in that last series,"' he told Ross. 'Now, what they don't realise is I'm trying to get a bit of pressure up – because of my age it's a bit tricky. Anyway, it wasn't working so I zipped up. I then told my son-in-law, "We're going to the loo again and you're going to come and protect me."' A fine anecdote, told with the ease and charm of a natural speaker. One could detect in his delivery the shy boy from east London, but that aspect only made the whole more appealing and real.

Matters of the body seem to be a recurring theme for Sugar's chat show repertoire and on a subsequent visit to Ross, he spoke amusingly of his latest health issues, climaxing in a graphic but entertaining punchline. 'I don't want to bore you with my medical history, but I had that groin problem,' he began. 'They fixed it in the end. I told you the last time I was here.' He then explained how the doctor who fixed his groin had expressed disbelief that Sir Alan had never had a colonoscopy.

What was that? wondered Ross and much of the audience.

'It's investigatory,' Sugar replied, before cutting straight to the chase. 'It's when they stick a camera up your backside, you know?'

He told how, when the doctor had done that, he had kept saying 'Ooh!' and 'Aah!' Sugar concluded, 'I thought he'd found Lord Lucan up there!'

Sugar's quip about his medical history is somewhat telling, as he has long been interested in his physical well being. Indeed, one of his childhood memories is of a physical ailment and the resulting treatment. 'It's a bad memory,' he sighs. 'I was six and I was dumped in this cot in Hackney Hospital to have my adenoids out. I screamed and shouted, saying I should be in a proper bed, not a cot, 'cos I was six. I was still screaming when they put the mask over my face. Afterwards, my mother promised me I'd never have to go to hospital again. She conned me. A year later, I was in the same hospital, having my tonsils out.'

Elsewhere, Sugar's light entertainment appearances have polarised critical opinion. In 2005, for instance, he appeared on BBC2's light-hearted *Room 101*, in which a celebrity guest is asked to nominate pet hates to be consigned to a fictional 'Room 101'. Hosted by Paul Merton, the show creates many funny moments as guests rant about their peculiar dislikes. With Sugar's reputation for grumpiness, the producers felt that they had a perfect guest. One of the things he chose was men who wear wigs. Hoping to add a bit of edge to proceedings, Merton showed Sugar a photograph of his US *Apprentice* equivalent Donald Trump. Sugar then promised a hilarious anecdote. He told Merton how while making an episode of *The Apprentice*, he had been filmed on a speedboat on the River Thames. 'I said to [the crew], "Trump couldn't do this," and they said, "Why not?" and I said, "'Cos his bloody hair would be back there at Tower Bridge."' It was not a classic anecdote and suffered all the more for the way Sugar had built it up.

Sugar received something of a roasting in the newspapers for his *Room 101* performance. In *The Times*, writer David Chater sneered: 'Prickly, glum and egotistical, Sir Alan Sugar is like Sid James without the laughs, and he makes Paul Merton struggle to generate any lightness or humour.'

Thomas Sutcliffe, of *The Independent*, was scarcely more impressed. He said: 'I know they'd never allow *Room 101* itself to be consigned to the chute but occasionally you get a guest who makes things a bit uncomfortable for a while and Sir Alan Sugar was one of them. You get the feeling that people don't interrupt Sir Alan's anecdotes often, so he has, to put it tactfully, evolved a notion of comic rhythm different than most people's. Listening to him dawdle through an underpowered story, the punchline of which was designed to show Sir Alan in a flattering light, Merton twitched with frustration, like a man in a Ferrari blocked in behind a steam roller.' Oh well, you can't win them all.

Interestingly, Sugar does not accept all requests for media spots. Even before his reality television fame, he was bombarded with offers of slots on the airwaves. Most were turned down, including the national radio institution *Desert Island Discs*.

One of Sugar's biggest successes in entertainment has been the public's introduction to the hugely popular Margaret Mountford through *The Apprentice*. The barrister's involvement with Sugar's business is a longstanding one. 'He was very different from the sort of client one had had before,' she admits. 'He questions everything and never accepts things just because he's told them. He's very commercial and always holds you to an estimate. Don't give an estimate of what your fees will be if you're working for him and think you can increase them at the end.'

His ideas and hers did not always agree during their making of *The Apprentice*, she says. Indeed, she believes it was the contrasting cultures that made for such a great dynamic behind the scenes. 'We have quite a long briefing session before the boardroom ... on who did well and who did badly. He takes our views into account. Sometimes we know who's going out – it's obvious. At other times it may be one of two. It depends on what he's looking for – whether it's someone good at sales, for instance, or a more managerial type of person. But someone whose sales technique he admires I'd probably never buy from. It's horses for courses.'

But it was very much in the frontline of proceedings that Mountford's presence was so keenly felt. She became a cult hero among *Apprentice* viewers who loved her quirky ways. As the *Irish News* noted: 'Silver-haired with piercing blue eyes, her armoury of expressive eye-rolling and disgusted sighs has effectively ruined the chances of several candidates, and her exchanges with fellow aide Nick Hewer have become some of the highlights of the series.'

The Irish newspaper was not alone in its admiration. As the *Guardian* put it, 'Mountford's signature look is the rolling of her eyes to heaven. Indeed, most of her loudest comments about the candidates are almost entirely nonverbal. The eye-rolling is frequently accompanied by a heartfelt sigh; in extremis, a sickened pursing of the lips. Her reaction to any act of stupidity is to drop her jaw in shock and amazement. Complete idiocy causes an additional flaring of the nostrils.'

Alex Clark of the *Observer* said that Mountford had

clear predecessors. 'Stella Rimington, Judi Dench, Stephanie Flanders (especially Stephanie Flanders) all have the same effect. Not Kirstie Allsopp, though, who attempts to carry off the same effect but looks like she might from time to time have a secret weep in a corner. Certainly, Mountford seems more suited to the task of whipping the rabble before her into shape than Sugar himself.'

Already a popular figure, Mountford's status soared in Series Four when she had a nation in stitches with her dry observation that Edinburgh University 'isn't what it used to be'.

Mountford was truly entertaining the nation, but with this came a level of fame that surprised and sometimes tested her. 'As a City lawyer you're pretty faceless outside the clients, the accountants, those you deal with. Now, people come up to me in the street, they feel they know me. I was walking along and someone said, "That's Alan Sugar's woman."

'I was very innocent about it really,' she says. 'The recognition took me by surprise. I don't mind when people come up and say, "Who's going to win?" But sometimes they invade your personal space. Say you're in a check-in queue, there's 25 minutes of queue ahead and the person next to you says, "You're from *The Apprentice,* aren't you?" They want to stand really close and go on and on about the series. I don't like that.'

When she stepped down from the show, the audience was heartbroken. Indeed when Sugar received his peerage soon after her retirement, some felt that perhaps he should leave television and leave the way open for her to return as the show's central figure. Mark Lawson of the *Guardian* wrote: 'Imagine her sweeping into the boardroom, receiving a cowed "Good morning, Mrs Mountford" from the ambitious wannabes. Never mind Lord Sugar, it's Lady Salt we need. One way or another, someone at the BBC must make it their challenge to get her back.'

Sugar's other sidekick, Nick Hewer, has also become something of a cult figure – again, a somewhat unlikely one. As the *Independent* said of him, 'With his silver, military haircut, frameless specs and deadpan intellect, Nick Hewer is not your average television star.' Hewer has been very defensive of the candidates who line up on the show each year, for he says he and Mountford personally understand why they might be feeling uncomfortable on the show.

'People have been reduced to nervous wrecks,' he says. 'Sugar's got this 20-second black stare, where his pupils appear to completely dilate and they go right through you and he's just silent. It's very unnerving. Margaret and I feel the tension, too. He doesn't tell us who he's going to fire or keep. And he's invariably got it right, over the whole series.'

The shy Sugar has also become used to dealing with the attention and fame *The Apprentice* has brought him. 'I don't mind it,' he said of seeing himself on the small screen. 'Yeah. I mean, I've been on television a lot. That's one of the reasons the BBC chose me because it's all very well finding a businessman but someone like Richard [Branson], who I know and admire very much, is just useless in front of the camera. He can't talk. That doesn't mean he's not a great businessman, but they needed someone who can talk. I've had years of doing TV interviews, both for Amstrad and in football, so I'm used to cameras.'

As a result of his fortune and fame, he has entertained himself with the odd expensive toy – mostly of the four-wheeled variety. A love of fine cars has motivated Sugar right back from his earliest business days in Hackney. 'What I was really after was wheels,' he said when asked why he first decided to go it alone in business, after taking several jobs. 'A car was considered to be an absolute luxury ... Rich people had cars – that's how you viewed it.'

He has since owned numerous posh cars, including the Rolls Royce Phantom that has become synonymous with *The Apprentice* star. So much so that when the model won an award, the press connected the honour with its most famous owner. *The Sun*'s headline was typical: SUGAR'S CAR IS SWEETEST MOTOR. When he began work in Westminster one newspaper claimed that his huge Bentley was causing problems in car parks as it took up two spaces and caused anxiety among other car park users that they might accidentally scratch it.

'There's only room for one big mouth in my organisation, and that's me,' Lord Sugar once said during an episode of *The Apprentice*. He can, on occasion, be similarly prickly away from the cameras, too. When Sugar and Rupert Murdoch were working on the development of Sky, the duo discussed how to best scramble the movie channel so only those paying for it would receive it. Sugar suggested using a smart card. Murdoch believed this would be too expensive but ultimately backed down when his own technical experts backed up Sugar's view. 'Don't start barking like an old crow and shouting your head off but basically you were right,' Murdoch told Sugar. 'We're going with the smart card.' However, he didn't hire Amstrad to make the smart cards. Instead he went with a rival firm. They'll deliver late, Sugar told Murdoch – and they did. One wonders whether he phoned Murdoch to tell him he told him so or not.

CHAPTER SEVEN
COURAGE

Of all the virtues in this section of the book, some would say that courage is the most important. Samuel Johnson would certainly agree with that. 'Courage is reckoned the greatest of all virtues,' he said, 'because unless a man has that virtue, he has no security for preserving any other.'

To reach his lofty position in the world and to keep his business empire going during good times and bad, Lord Sugar has shown plenty of bravery. Right from the start when he eschewed the example of his father and went it alone in his working life he has shown he has a brave, British heart. Never was this more evident than during his time in football. It is a brave man who voluntarily incurs the wrath of football fans by denying them a golden-boy hero such as Terry Venables as a manager. Lord Sugar is such a man. To understand how and why he came to make such a courageous decision, we should look at how he came to be involved in the game of football.

Tottenham Hotspur were already £4 million in debt when owner Irving Scholar appointed Douglas Alexiou as chairman. Sadly, this was not enough to stop the continuing slide. As the 1980s turned into the 1990s Scholar was desperate to find a way to get the club back on its feet again. Initially he turned to newspaper magnate Robert Maxwell. Although he only asked Maxwell for funds, his approach prompted an even bigger response: Maxwell made a bid to buy the club. This put him in a straight head-to-head battle with Alan Sugar, who was, by this time, preparing a takeover bid of his own. As a youngster, he had been taken by his father to watch the team play at White Hart Lane. Then, in the 1980s, the Amstrad office was based in Garman Road, just around the corner from Spurs' stadium. He had even once used the Tottenham team in an advertising campaign for Amstrad.

Sugar's bid for the club in June 1991 was launched in partnership with football manager Terry Venables. Venables had enjoyed a successful playing career, joining Chelsea as an apprentice, quickly becoming a first-team regular and then club captain, leading the team to victory in the League Cup in 1965. However, a year later he was sold to Tottenham Hotspur, where he was part of the team that won the FA Cup in 1967. Their opponents?

Chelsea. He was a success as a manager too. He took Crystal Palace to two successive promotions and then moved across town to Queens Park Rangers, where he led them to the Division Two title.

Clubs around the world noted his managerial success and he was soon signed up by one of the biggest: FC Barcelona. He led the Catalan club to its first league title in 11 years, a League Cup win and a European Cup Final, which they lost on penalties. Soon he had earned himself a new nickname: 'El Tel'. It turned bitter for him, though, and in September 1987, not long after Barcelona had twice lost to Dundee United in the UEFA Cup quarter-finals, he was sacked. Just two months later he was given the manager's seat at Tottenham Hotspur and his fateful path-crossing with Sugar was about to occur.

The pair made a striking contrast. 'Terry is all charm, he could persuade you that black is white,' said a businessman who had worked with both. 'Alan is gruff and aggressive. But both have monster egos and their self-belief is rarely shaken.'

Given that their partnership was to be an essentially business rather than football-based one, it is instructive to quote the words of a journalist who wrote of Sugar's superior experience in the field, saying: 'In this world, Alan Michael Sugar is AC Milan. And Terry Venables is Halifax Town.'

Not that Venables was without business experience – or controversy in that field. A man who has had widespread business interests for many years, Venables has strongly denied allegations of financial impropriety made against him. Yet in January 1998 he was banned from holding company directorships for seven years after choosing not to contest 19 specific allegations made against him by the Department of Trade and Industry. The case concerned allegations of mismanagement of four companies.

Venables has also become known in areas other than playing for and managing football clubs. He co-wrote novels with author Gordon Williams and co-created the '70s detective series *Hazell* television series for ITV, based on those books. His other extra-curricular projects include creating a football board game, *Terry Veneables Invites You To Become... The Manager*, and appearing on a 2002 World Cup pop song, Rider's *England Crazy*, which reached number 46 in the UK singles charts. Having courted the football press for some years, the tanned, charismatic Venables had become a popular figure among many newspaper writers, who competed with each other to write glowing profiles of him. This, together with his popularity among football fans, made him a formidable enemy to take on, as Sugar would soon learn.

As the joint Sugar/Venables bid came up against the one from Maxwell, Sugar was straightforward. 'I can't deny that Terry and I have made an approach to the board of Tottenham Hotspur and we are awaiting the outcome of that offer. If Mr Maxwell or any other party wish to come along for the benefit of the club and put forward proposals which are better than I am, I will gracefully step to one side because one thing that is not going to happen is an auction,' he said. Showing the sort of sales qualities that had been noted since his schooldays, Sugar said: 'I've got a cheque in the fridge and Terry Venables and I are ready to go as soon as the board sorts itself out. We put serious proposals to the board on Monday and I believe that with Terry's undisputed talent and history of success combined with my financial backing, the future prospects for Spurs are excellent.' It seemed a strong pitch.

However, the matter dragged on, forcing Sugar to publicly pressure Tottenham Hotspur into siding with him. 'We have heard a lot of noise about another possible bid for Spurs,' he said, before turning to Maxwell's other football interests, which included ownership of Derby County. 'Our reading of the concisely written League rules means that even if Derby are sold, Robert Maxwell still cannot bid for Spurs. His family holding in Oxford and Reading would have to be disposed of first, unless the League gives written dispensation. I cannot believe that the League could find sufficient reason to do so in the light of our solid bid and the known feelings of the fans, players and many small shareholders, all of whom desperately want Terry Venables to stay on.'

The co-ordinator of a leading Tottenham fan group

backed Sugar's words, vowing, 'We would be prepared to take legal advice to seek an injunction if it seemed the league was going to break its own rules.'

It was not just among day-to-day fans that Sugar's bid was favoured. Frank Sinclair, one of Tottenham's executive directors, told the press, 'We are pleased about any bid that's likely to be successful. The club has received numerous approaches over the last nine months, but the important thing is to have one that is likely to have a successful outcome. Mr Sugar has considerable financial muscle.' At 46th in the *Sunday Times* Rich List, with £157 million to his name, he did indeed have that muscle.

The tide seemed to be running strongly in Sugar's favour, with one (unnamed) Spurs boardroom member telling the *Independent* that as far as he was concerned, Sugar was the man to pick: 'For the first time in many months of negotiation, Venables has finally come up with someone who has got the money involved. Alan Sugar is a very bright fellow. We can do business with him.' Asked why Sugar would want to get involved in football, the source was unsure. 'Who knows? Maybe he's got tired of computer games and wants a new toy. He can afford it.'

Sugar, however, was quite clear about the attraction of the deal. 'Look, this is the fourth time I've told you,' the Sugar told one persistent inquisitor. 'It's a business proposition and a very good business proposition.'

Sugar had one final blast on his own trumpet via the media, again singing the praises of his co-bidder

Venables. Here, he played clearly to the emotions of the fans. Speaking of the benefits of his bid, he played the Venables card and phrased his words as if their bid had already won. 'I think the supporters will really be very, very pleased that Terry Venables is still involved with the club. I think that is the key issue.'

On Saturday 22 June, the Sugar/Venables bid won. The pair called a triumphant press conference to announce that they had reached agreement with the board and the Stock Exchange to take control of Tottenham Hotspur. Sugar would be non-executive chairman of the company with the task of 'getting the balance sheet into shape' while Venables would take over the role of managing director. They immediately paid off the club's £20 million debt and everything seemed set for a bright future under the guidance of what many believed would be the dream team. How wrong they were.

In May 1993, Sugar sacked Venables. At the end of a fiery two-hour meeting, Venables emerged clearly shaken and said: 'The board has voted to dismiss me and I have been and am talking to solicitors. I am advised that's all I can say at the moment.'

Sugar said the decision was not taken as a result of matters on the field – where Tottenham were doing reasonably well – but due to some of Venables's businesses. 'Nobody is questioning his ability as a football coach. And it was a very sad day on Friday and everybody involved regrets deeply that it has come to this.'

He later expanded on this, and pointed the way to the future. 'Obviously fans want the team to be strong, they want good management of the football side. We have got good management there at the moment, which worked under Terry Venables: Doug Livermore and Ray Clemence. We will apply the funds in an appropriate manner that one should apply cash in a football club. And the playing will tell the story. Fans are very fickle. There is a distinct possibility that three or four games into the season, if we win and the manager becomes a hero, the cruel harsh reality is that maybe, maybe Terry is forgotten.'

Later still, he said: 'I'd like to say to the fans that I and the board have the best interests of the club at heart. This is not an ego trip – I'm not an egotistical loony. If I was I'd have been reported many times before for interfering in football. This club has been established since 1882. It's bigger than me, it's bigger than Robert Maxwell and it's bigger than Terry Venables.'

Although he was correct in saying the club was bigger than Venables, Sugar was under no illusions as to how unpopular his decision would be. Venables was enormously popular within football, and nowhere was this popularity stronger than among fans of Tottenham Hotspur: as a former player and manager he was considered one of their own. Football fans can form a brutal and unforgiving force. Once their ire is raised they can be terrifying to whoever is on their wrong side. The money men involved in the game have never been people who naturally attract much respect from fans at the best of times. Even when one is at the helm of a period of great success, it is normally the manager and players who are credited with bringing the good times to the club. So when things are not going well, it is easy to blame the financial figures, and when the man at the top has personally taken a difficult and unpopular decision, he is asking for trouble.

Sugar had been brave, but not unthinking. Looking back at his decision, he said: 'Terry: clever man, wise man, smart fellow, written books, loved by the fans. Some people would have said, "No, I'm not gonna take on God's gift." But I made a statement: I was in, up to here. Terry Venables was out. I made that statement to the world at large, to my family, to me.'

He knew his decision to kick out 'God's gift' was to bring trouble – and it did. Venables took the case to the High Court, applying for an injunction against the dismissal. He won a temporary reprieve, but the judge ruled that reinstating Venables would 'merely postpone the date at which all concerned must face up to the fact that his appointment, for better or worse, has been terminated'.

Spurs fans were furious and chanted 'We want Sugar out!' in front of court. Sugar was escorted out of a back door and has since said that in firing Venables he felt like he had murdered Bambi. Venables, who lost the subsequent three-day High Court case and was ordered to pay costs, has been surprisingly conciliatory towards Sugar since. 'I don't know what would have happened to the club without him,' he has acknowledged. 'He was the only one prepared to go through with it.'

Sugar had needed all his courage in order to get through the court case, aided throughout by barrister Margaret Mountford. She recalls the strain that the case brought to Sugar. 'The court case ... should never have happened. It should've been thrown out,' she said. 'I advised Alan he was entitled to sack Venables and I was right.

'But it was horrible for him, the acrimony and personal hostility he suffered ... Some fans, in my opinion, are little better than savages. It's very tribal.' Using the charm and fine turn of phrase that would later make her so popular on television, Mountford recalled how tough it was for herself and Sugar to arrive at court each day. 'The fans were ghastly. You had to go past these awful spitting yobs on the way in and out of court, which is not what one is accustomed to as a City solicitor.'

A few years later Sugar would need to show his courage once more, but this time he was leading the way for Tottenham fans to follow, as the club faced a very testing period. The Football Association had for some time been investigating suggestions that illegal payments had been made by the club to players during the 1980s, long before Sugar was involved. In June 1994 the investigation was completed and the club found guilty. The punishment was fierce: 12 league points were to be deducted for the following campaign, the club would be banned from the FA Cup for the same season and it was fined £600,000.

The club's public response was unsurprising: 'The board of Tottenham Hotspur is extremely disappointed and unhappy at yesterday's decision by the Football Association and is considering options available to it and will make a decision by the end of next week as to what action, if any, to take.'

That was the public response. It is fair to speculate that Sugar's words behind closed doors were more direct. This was a terrible blow to the club's hopes. Football commentators immediately speculated that Tottenham would not only finish next season trophy-less but having just finished only four points clear of the drop, they would also find themselves relegated from the top flight.

The club immediately appealed and received good and bad news from the hearing. The bad was that the fine was increased to £1.5 million and the FA Cup ban was upheld, but the points deduction was reduced from 12 to six points. It was a dark hour for the club, with both fans and players crestfallen before the season even began. Sugar here showed himself to be a courageous leader as he rallied all concerned.

'We're not going down,' he said after the points deduction was reduced to six. 'We have just lost two games, that's all. Looking on the positive side, when

Arsenal had points deducted in 1991, they went on to win the Championship.'

Sugar also looked for ways to get the punishment further softened. To do this he reminded the football authorities that the game was rife with corruption and that by punishing Tottenham they had hardly scratched the surface of what was going on inside the game. This was not the sort of territory that cowards could tread in, which was why Sugar excelled. 'I don't want to be dragged down to the levels of depravity which may exist in the football industry in hiding or covering up things. So I hope the private arbitration in this case will find for honesty, because that's always the best policy,' he said. He also continued to up the ante and tighten the pressure on the FA. 'I'm sorry if the tribunal holds up what the Football Association has done. I will use my best endeavours on behalf of the shareholders of my club to disclose the same irregularities by other clubs. It doesn't matter who they are. I make that quite clear because if we are treated that way and I find it has happened at other clubs, they should be treated the same.'

His campaign continued with an interview in which he expanded on what he felt was hypocrisy in the way Spurs had been dealt with. 'To me, when you see the ratbags in football, it's commendable that there's a regulatory body like the Football Association which still holds it all together. But common sense tells you whatever Tottenham are supposed to be guilty of, if the same misdemeanour was perpetrated by Brighton and Hove Albion, there's no way they would have been fined £1.5 million.' He felt that the club was being punished especially heavily because of its (relative) wealth. 'I'm rich, OK, but if I park my Rolls-Royce in Kensington, the fine is 30 quid, the same as it would be for someone with a bubble car. The FA have stuck a finger in the air and said, "Right, it's Tottenham, they've got plenty of money." Wallop.'

The pressure he was applying seemed to work. The second appeal hearing led to both the deduction of points and the FA Cup ban being withdrawn. Sugar was in triumphant and bullish mood. Having had the Venables saga and then the punishment scandal overshadow his time in football, he stood up for himself proudly in the wake of the appeal. 'The rumours are that I'm so arrogant, so set in my ways, that I'm not prepared to admit I'm wrong,' he said. 'That's a load of balderdash. I'm known in the business world as a cut-and-run man. I'm not proud to admit to mistakes, but I've made them and I'm out before you know it.

'I've got faith that the truth, honesty and that straight dealing will out in the end,' he added. 'Believe me when I tell you that if I hadn't volunteered the information about what happened here in the past, none of this would be happening to Spurs. I don't regret doing what I've done because that would be going against my nature. And if I was like the way I'm portrayed in the press – as this nasty villainous ogre, which has really upset me and my family – don't you think I would have been exposed by now?'

His fine mood was shared by the club's supporters. When they had called for his head and subjected him to a campaign of hate over the sacking of Venables, Sugar had bravely soaked up the abuse and waited for his chance to win them over. Finally, he had done so. The writer Norman Fox summed up the mood in the *Independent*: 'Watch Sugar at a match now and you see a fan. Most chairmen wince a little when the opposition score and smile reservedly when their own team do so. Sugar grimaces and roars.'

Fox was not alone in noticing this. The *Evening Standard*'s leading football writer Michael Herd wrote, 'What has happened to Alan Sugar? Has he picked up the [Blackburn Rovers owner] Jack Walker virus and given himself up to football, body and soul? Has Mr Grumpy got the bug, despite everything he's seen and heard in the past three years? After all, it wasn't so long ago he was telling us his association with Tottenham was his single biggest mistake. He'd gone to White Hart Lane as a boy but since then he hadn't shown any interest in football.'

Successive displays of courage had helped win the fans over to the charms and vision of Sugar. However, it would be wrong to suggest that all his brave decisions in football were quite so successful. The fourth manager appointed under Sugar's reign was Christian Gross, virtually unknown outside his native Switzerland in spite of winning two Swiss titles with Grasshoppers Zurich. True, Frenchman Arsene Wenger was also almost unknown in Britain before his appointment at Arsenal the year before, but Gross was to prove no Wenger, and Sugar's appointment backfired on him.

In truth, the writing was on the wall before Gross had taken charge of a single match in north London. When Sugar proudly unveiled his new managerial appointment at a press conference, the resulting performance from Gross was memorable. Gross kicked-off proceedings by waving a London Underground ticket at the surprised journalists. 'I wanted to know the way the fans will come to White Hart Lane,' he said, to widespread amusement. 'I needed to show that I am one of them. This is a big, big job, a big, big challenge. I hope this is the ticket to my dream.' Sitting alongside a nodding Sugar, Gross added: 'I have to stop the fall. That means good team spirit, discipline inside and outside the team, and bringing in a new system.'

The smartly dressed Gross was clearly a disciplinarian. 'I was a team player,' he roared. 'Team-work was very important. For me there must be that spirit. If you have discipline, you are powerful. Players have to be disciplined.' Heads were shaken not just among the journalists, but also among the fans of the club. Sure enough, Gross proved an unsuccessful manager and he was soon buying a new London Underground ticket, to start him on the journey home.

It had been a brave – but unwise – decision to give Gross the manager's seat. However, the man who Sugar had lined up to replace him was to prove such a jaw-dropping choice that nobody could dispute Sugar's balls in giving him the job. After a short period with former manager David Pleat back in charge as a caretaker boss, Sugar was ready to unveil the new manager. It was an appointment that shook football. Sugar might not have been a football fanatic but he knew his stuff and was therefore well aware that the man he had in mind was going to be a very controversial choice.

George Graham is a man steeped in Arsenal's history. He had joined the Gunners as a player in 1966 and become a key part of the team. Popular among the fans, he was nicknamed 'Stroller' for his sometimes languid style of play. In 1971 he starred for Arsenal as they won the league and FA Cup double, the first time the club had won both honours in the same campaign. After retiring from playing, Graham became a manager. This surprised some, because his style of play was so laidback that he did not instantly exude the sort of nature that would lend itself to the application required of a manager. However, he answered his critics by becoming a fantastic success with a solid reputation as a disciplinarian – so much so that some players nicknamed him 'Gadaffi' after the hardline leader of Libya.

Graham returned to Arsenal in the late 1980s as manager, leading the north London giants – and fierce rivals of Tottenham – to numerous trophies, including the league championship, FA Cup and European Cup Winners' Cup. This caused misery among the Tottenham fans: watching their bitterest rivals winning trophy after trophy while they won precious little was painful. The fans' only comfort was that Graham's managerial style produced teams that often sacrificed flair for success. As Arsenal fans boasted of their team's success, Tottenham fans would respond with derisive chants of 'Boring, boring Arsenal'. Their belief that Tottenham's tradition was to play a more attractive style of football was the one thing they had left over Arsenal fans.

So when Sugar announced that the next manager of Tottenham was to be none other than George Graham, the fans were up in arms. Sugar tried to reason with them as he unveiled his man at the press conference. 'If you work for IBM or Ford you would go for the best in the field, someone who has been successful. George is one of, if not *the*, top manager in English football. Why has he come to Tottenham? Results, that's the end of it.' It was a brave stance to take. For Spurs fans the results were not the only thing that concerned them. They also wanted football played what they considered 'the right way' – and they did not believe that Graham was the man to deliver that. And besides, he was an Arsenal man and therefore a sworn enemy of the club.

Sugar confidently ploughed on with backing Graham. 'The single most important man at a football club is the manager. Maybe we will start a trend here but it should have happened a long time ago. We must never sit on the edge of our seats again wondering whether we will be relegated. If George is not successful we should have to examine the reasons why. We will have to see if the place is doomed, I'm jinxed, or that we might have to get an exorcist in ... or even [faith healer] Eileen Drewery. But the fact is we have not performed for the fans at all. We have not given them anything to cheer about. Some managers come in and wave cheque books about and others get spontaneous results. George is consistently a winner and in any walk of life you have got to get those kind of people around you.'

Assured words, but as ever he was under no illusions as to the risk he had taken. Just as he had faced flack for sacking Venables, he knew he would receive plenty more for his appointment of Graham. 'I have passed my sell-by date in the eyes of the fans but it's time to get this club in shape and performing well, give it the status it deserves. But there is a limit to the thickness of a rhino's skin and I won't put up with the abuse from the fans. It's just not worth it. However, I am in no frame of mind to think about selling out, it's as simple as that.

'But I like to work in an environment where there is a goal at the end of the rainbow or that your efforts are appreciated. The fans are part of our team here and in appointing George I believe the board have made an excellent choice. Anything I do, in any companies that I own, you work as a team and your efforts are appreciated. Having been branded cynical and a cold person who has no knowledge of football or interest in the heritage and tradition of the club, you spend seven years trying to convince people it's not the case and in the end you go with the flow.'

Sugar continued to receive plenty of abuse for his choice of manager for some time after Graham's arrival. Indeed, many never forgave him for bringing Graham to the club – even after the Scot led Spurs to their first trophy in eight years, beating Leicester City in the League Cup final. For some the fact that 'an Arsenal man' had been responsible for the victory paled the joy.

In other corners, however, Sugar was praised for his courage and leadership. at Spurs' director of football, David Pleat, was gracious enough to praise the chairman amid the celebrations at the end of the victorious final. 'Now it's time for Alan to sit back and enjoy it. The chairman has gained experience from the first few years. Early on he had a few problems not of his making as there was no one on the board with a football background. Very often mediocre players were signed. Very often cover was needed for injuries and sometimes players were bought on a whim simply as cover when they weren't really up to it. Now there is confidence in the management and I'm there to provide information and keep the chairman in touch. He is a hands-on chairman and rightly so. He should be aware of everything that happens at his football club.'

Soon, though, the hate campaign against Sugar became too much for those who really mattered to him – his family. 'We had people outside the house, holding up banners,' said Sugar's wife Ann. 'It was just awful. It was awful for the kids to see as well. I kept saying to Alan, "Why did you get involved in this world?" It was just awful.'

The hands-on chairman was eventually to take his hands off and leave the club, a move he announced in 2000 in typical straightforward style. 'No jokes. No tricks, I'm off. And I will do it in a professional manner,' he said. 'The company has made an announcement to the Stock Exchange that we are in talks with various people. As soon as any of these become statutory and reportable we shall comment on them. There are no deals right now. But, as they say, we are hot to trot.'

In the event Sugar stepped down the following year after selling up to leisure club ENIC. He had enjoyed an eventful ten years in football, but sadly he left with few happy memories and even fewer positive things to say about his experiences in the so-called beautiful game. 'You could forgive Alan Sugar for renaming Tottenham's ground White Hart Strain after his troubled tenure as Spurs chairman,' commented a BBC journalist.

It was a sentiment that Sugar would readily agree with. Later on he looked back at his football experience with regret – not just at what he encountered in the game, but also for the effect it had on his business. 'What went wrong was, I think, my persistence in thinking that perhaps I could make it a successful business and also successful on the football pitch,' he said. 'What went wrong is my poor reading of the situation. After year in, year out trying to do things that way, what went wrong was it took me too long to realise that I was pissing in the wind, literally wasting my time, banging my head up against the wall. That's what went wrong. My fault. It was a waste of my life.

'I think a clever person, a clever outside observer who wants to do a commercial analysis on me, should track Amstrad's results throughout the course of that ten years, then track them now. After I leave Tottenham and get back to concentrating on Amstrad, you start to see the profits rising again. And that tells a story. No one's picked up on that really. The story is, I suppose, I'm a one-horse/pony man or whatever you want to call it. When I give my attention to something I tend to give it all and I think in hindsight that, apart from me losing ten years out of my life, Amstrad shareholders actually lost me for a while. I took my eye off the ball for a wasted, hopeless, ungrateful bunch of people.'

He had been surprised by the ability of pundits to fill up hours of airtime on football television shows and the way their views were given such automatic reverence. He found this to be a big contrast to how business broadcasting went, for instance.

'In other walks of life, when expressing something on TV or in a newspaper, you are bound by strict guidelines,' he said. 'The Trade Descriptions Act is one that comes to mind. Companies are not allowed to mislead people with wild claims. But in football it seems anything goes.'

As an example, Sugar mentioned how former Arsenal star Frank McLintock had spoken out against Spurs' sacking of George Graham, giving 'what he has done for the club' as evidence of the sacking being wrong. 'Well, in the time he was manager, Graham spent more money than any other boss in Spurs' history,' Sugar said. 'He also spent more money in the period of time he was at Spurs than he did at any other club. And what did he achieve for this outlay of cash? The Worthington Cup, that's what.'

Sugar was fuming at McLintock's comment. 'It makes me sick to sit and listen to these distorted comments. And what makes it worse is you, the punters, are asked to believe that rubbish. As a viewer or reader you've got no chance of hearing a balanced view and it's presented to you like a Bambi of the football world has been shot.'

Sugar was no fan of football journalists. Having crossed swords with Graham and Venables, both charismatic men with many toadying contacts in the media, he had faced numerous hostile reports in the printed press. He summed up his feelings about the men who wrote the reports thus: 'If they talked long enough, they could even convince you that Gary Lineker had tiny ears.'

It is a shame that Sugar so regrets his time in the game, although it is understandable given the abuse he faced from fans and the rampant disloyalty he found among the players. Even after he had left, he still came in for stick, not least from the man he so bravely gave a job at Spurs – George Graham. The Scot continued to blame Sugar for the club's woes, even long after he had stepped down.

'George Graham is very experienced at playing the media game, orchestrating the press with a clever quote or an easy headline,' sighed Sugar. 'Unfortunately, many fans can't see through this little trick unless someone like me spells it out. But let me ask you something: Have you ever noticed nothing is ever George Graham's fault? And I mean *nothing*. Now how can that be true? None of us is perfect, yet George has cleverly mastered the art of deflection and is very successful at diverting attention from himself and his failings.' He joked that if footage was found of George Graham robbing a bank, it would be blamed not on him but on Alan Sugar. He concluded: 'Graham is a gutless coward who will not stand up and admit he has made mistakes. In my time at Tottenham I made lots of mistakes: the biggest was possibly employing him.'

Talk about having the last laugh. Sugar has a retort for anything those in the game try and throw at him. Heaven help any Spurs fan who tries to dismiss what Sugar brought to their club, for he has a fine way with words and is entirely at ease with his contribution. 'I took Del Boy's stall and turned it into Marks & Spencer,' he told one such fan. Will the Tottenham faithful ever – en masse – take a clear-eyed look at the enormous contribution that Sugar brought to their club? He won't be holding his breath.

Let's leave this episode in sugar's life on a positive note: 'Whether you believe it or not, I love Tottenham Hotspur Football Club and I've only ever wanted the best for it,' he said. In seeking the best for the club he had been forced to endure some highly unpleasant times. In facing them he had displayed the sort of courage that few of his enemies could justifiably claim for themselves.

Lord Sugar's courage has shown itself numerous times throughout his life. When he launched AmsAir, he shook up the prevailing method of operating in the private jet industry, as his son Daniel explained. 'It's the attention to detail that gives someone the leading edge. Rather than being price-led, the big corporates prefer to use us because we get the service right. Our tailor-made package is really a bit different to our competitors.'

In his property dealings, too, Sugar has proved himself to be a brave man. He once did a controversial deal for some Old Park Lane property. He recalls that the agent told him in an Eton accent that he would never secure the prices he wanted for the apartments in the property. 'I said to him, in my Hackney accent, with a few expletives added, that when the right person comes along and falls in love with the place then they'll pay anything for it. That's exactly what happened.' Oh, the sweet taste of vindication!

Sugar's courage has not always been vindicated as much as he would have hoped, however. One of the more disappointing products that Sugar launched was the 'E-mailer' telephone, brought out in 1999 – a phone that also allowed the customer to send emails. , It was a bold move at the early stage of the home-technology trend. At the launch, Sugar said: 'I see the E-mailer becoming the "all-in-one communications centre" in the home. It will also be regarded as an "electronic billboard", providing advertisers with a highly cost-effective way of targeting consumers. In true Amstrad tradition the E-mailer brings e-mail to the mass market for the first time in an easy-to-use format at a very affordable price.' The E-mailer was to cost the customer £79.99.

The early response was not overwhelming and more than 17 per cent was wiped off the value of Amstrad shares on the day of the launch. One City analyst said: 'The group's new E-mailer product may well be a winner, but it would have to be something spectacular to have justified all the hype which has been surrounding this company for several months now.'

Sugar attempted to brush aside the growing negativity, insisting that the 'City scribblers' had got it wrong. 'I am not ready to be put out to grass yet,' he said. 'We have launched enough products over 25 years to know which ones are going to fly off the shelves. You can tell from customers' reaction very early on whether a new product is going to be a winner.' The first batch of 500 E-mailer phones had sold out within two days, he said. However, the sceptics in the media seemed to scent blood.

'Sir Alan Sugar's Amstrad has sold nearly 5,000 E-mailers a week since it went on general sale early this summer,' said the *Daily Mail*. 'But the heavily-subsidised sales, of 70,000 units so far, come at a heavy cost. They knocked £2.3 million off profits in the June year and the costs continue.'

Two years after the launch, Sugar was still bravely defending his E-mailer. 'People say I'm nuts, but the E-mailer is cheap and useful as a phone, before you consider everything else it can do.'

To be fair, the picture did subsequently improve. 'Amstrad back in black as E-mailer sales improve,' cheered the *Financial Times* in September 2003 as Amstrad halved the price of the unit.

A spokesman explained the pricing decision: 'The business model is fine but we need more sales.' Commercial director Simon Sugar said, 'The price reduction will be supported by press advertising and in-store promotions and we are confident that this will increase sales significantly. We have had nearly three years' experience of running the E-mailer business and the revenue per phone has held up well.'

To this day the E-mailer is regularly damned as a spectacular failure, but the raw data does not support this. Amstrad sold almost 298,000 units and claimed a million users during its first four years of existence. Benefiting from increased subscription revenues and lower production costs, the division turned a £5.5 million loss into a £1 million profit on sales of £6.5 million.

However, the media would need a lot of convincing. 'JURY STILL OUT ON SIR ALAN'S GADGET,' said the *Daily Telegraph* in 2004. The jury might be out, but Sugar delivered his own verdict of what happened when the dotcom bubble burst.

'We launched the first E-mailer in the middle of all that internet bullshit, and when it started to collapse we got dragged down with it. The one thing I learned is that money talks. OK? We are in profit now. That answers all the doubters. We will continue to increase profits. That's the bottom line. You can talk about all that future technology crap, but we are actually in profit and you can't argue with the facts.'

By the beginning of 2006, however, the facts showed that the E-mailer was not firing on all cylinders. 'SUGAR'S E-MAILER IN THE FIRING LINE AS PROFITS FALL,' said the *Guardian* in February. Later that year Amserve stopped making the product. 'SUGAR CANED AS PLUG PULLED ON E-MAILER' said the *Evening Standard*. All the same, his launching and perseverance with the product again showed his courage. You cannot win them all, and Lord Sugar did not lose with the E-mailer to the extent suggested.

If Sugar had to show bravery in the harsh and unforgiving world of business, then that went double for him as he entered the rough and tumble environment of British politics. He was not scared to take on those who took him on. For instance, when the Conservative shadow culture secretary Jeremy Hunt was so vocal about his appointment as a Labour peer, he bit back ferociously, accusing him of acting 'high and mighty'. Hunt returned to the theme in December, asking questions in the House about how many times Sugar had visited Lord Mandelson's Department for Business, Innovation and Skills since his appointment. The answer was that he had visited more than 40 times. 'However,' said Pat McFadden, minister of state at the department in question, 'the main focus of his work as Enterprise Champion has been meeting small businesses and seeing business support delivery around the country.'

A few days later Sugar took another bite out of Hunt, who had been shown to have broken expenses rules. Tory leader David Cameron had received praise from some for his response to the expenses scandal, and in May 2009 he called on all MPs to apologise. 'It's not good enough to say we obeyed the rules,' he said. 'We need a big acknowledgement that we are sorry that this happened and it needs to change.'

Sugar dared Cameron to sack Hunt, saying that his bid for electoral victory could not be taken seriously otherwise. 'The man [Hunt] has problems understanding rules and regulations,' Sugar said. 'If Cameron is to have any hope of being taken seriously next year as a contender, he has to rid himself of people like Hunt.'

Politics is not an environment for the shrinking violet and Sugar is hardly one of those. It is hard to not get excited at the thought of more clashes of words between him and his political opponents. If anyone has the honesty and bravery to thrive in that gladiatorial arena then it is Lord Sugar.

PART THREE

A FINE FUTURE?

What does the future hold for Lord Sugar? As he progresses through his sixties, he reaches the age when most men retire. To say that Sugar is unlikely to settle down in front of the fire with a pipe and slippers is not a shocking revelation to any student of his life story, but what might he do during the coming years?

In business his options are open. He is now free from Amstrad, having sold it to BSkyB in 2007. The fee? A brilliant £125 million. Nearly 40 years previously he had started the company from humble roots; he has now sold it for a fortune and was delighted with the deal. Could he ever have imagined back then how his business would have progressed?

At the time of the sale, he said: 'I cannot imagine a better home for the Amstrad business and its talented people. Our companies share the entrepreneurial spirit of bringing innovation to the largest number of customers. Sky is a great British success story. I'm proud to have worked so closely with it, and I look forward to continuing to play a part in this exciting business.'

James Murdoch of BSkyB was also delighted with the deal. 'Sky and Amstrad have had a long and positive relationship,' he said. 'The acquisition accelerates supply chain improvement and will help us to drive innovation and efficiency for the benefit of our customers.' The deal was worth £34 million to Sir Alan personally and capped a very profitable period for him. The previous month, he had sold his Tottenham Hotspur shares for £25 million.

When Sugar expanded on where he saw himself and Amstrad, he gave a hint of how he sees himself in his senior days. 'I turned 60 this year: I've done 40 years of hustling in this business. I have to start thinking about my team of loyal staff, many of whom have been around me for a very long time. There's a certain culture there that will exist. It's not a case of letting it go, it's a case of moving the company on to something more positive ... The good news for my employees is that they've now got a secure future with great opportunities. The bad news is that I'm still going to be around for a while, so nothing changes at Amstrad.' The following year he was no longer around, after formally stepping down from the fray.

'This is a move that has been planned for a while and it's the right time for me to step down from my role at Amstrad,' he explained. 'The past 40 years have seen

Amstrad grow from a start-up business to the success story that it is today, which is credit to the talented and loyal team here. I have decided that it is the right time to step back from my role at Amstrad.'

The reigns were handed to Amstrad's managing director Alun Webber. Sugar praised him, saying: 'Alun has worked closely with Amstrad over a number of years and is the right person to build on the success that we have seen to date. I step back knowing that the company's future is in good hands.'

Meanwhile, Lord Sugar's hands became free to turn to new fields and to face new challenges. He is under no illusions about the feelings of many in politics over his presence in that sphere, but if anything this will only encourage him to remain and thrive. 'There is a little bit of an antagonistic presence here,' he told the *Daily Telegraph*'s Celia Walden after the ceremony that saw him formally become a peer. 'Not from the staff, who have welcomed me with open arms, or from a nice, select group of the peers, but I do feel that some of the members think I am a villain from the telly. They have this image of me as a brusque, ignorant cockney but I have been underestimated many times in my career and I have always proved people wrong. During the ceremony, I only got a mild "hear, hear" – mostly from the Labour lot.' Walden recalled that a 'flicker of resentment' shot across his face at this point. He then added, 'But they'll like me in the end.'

Sugar has certainly ruffled some feathers in the political world. During the aforementioned interview, Sugar's mobile telephone rang. He and Walden were in the august surroundings of the peers' dining room at the time and the sound of Sugar's phone prompted disgusted looks from across the room. 'Look,' he laughed. 'I'll get 20 lashes. But you know what? They'll get used to me. I am good for the Lords. Besides, I'm doing it for the people – I'm the people's Lord.' How typical of Sugar's approach to life to care not about so much the peers as about his own – the people. So he returned, with a shrug, to his lunch. His down-to-earth honesty once again polarises opinion of the man. Some soak it up, finding it a refreshing change in a world of fakery. Others, in truth, find it too much and overbearing.

Sugar cares little about their feelings. It is little wonder some in the cosseted surroundings of Westminster might fear or even resent a man who has earned every penny of his fortune, and deserves all the influence, power and fame that came as a result. Hereditary peers might share a chamber with him but they are, after all, the polar opposite of Sugar, and he does not support their continued appointment. 'No, frankly I don't agree with that,' he snaps. 'But there are actually very few now and although there are people here who have achieved a lot and are brilliant in their fields, there are also people who have done absolutely nothing.' The latter camp will, in all likelihood, always resent Sugar's place in their world.

But he is there to stay, whether on the benches or beyond. Lord Sugar is now a political figure, the people's peer, and that is how he will remain. He has stayed in touch with where he came from – and the people who still live there – throughout his rise to wealth and power.

Sugar's success as a businessman is in large part down to this quality. In the 1970s it was he who breathed fresh air through the hi-fi market. He was not aiming his products primarily at the musical geeks who were obsessed with minute developments in technology. Instead he wanted to sell his products to the ordinary man and woman who just wanted equipment that would play their pop records well. For this target market Sugar came up with a down-to-earth and succinct description: 'the truck driver and his wife'. He made his fortune with this common-sense approach.

So how might this multi-millionaire live out the remainder of his years?

We can look to other business tycoons for hints of how his life might look. For instance, Andrew Carnegie, the Scottish captain of industry who created US Steel and made himself a billionaire in the process. He retired in his late sixties and turned to philanthropy. He also wrote two books: *Triumphant Democracy* and *Gospel of Wealth*. By the time he died he had given away the equivalent of over $4 billion. John D Rockefeller, too, was a philanthropist in his later years and lived to the ripe age of 97 – just three years short of the magic 100 that he had dreamed of reaching since a child.

Lord Sugar is currently planning to write his autobiography and has proven, as we have seen, an enormously generous man. His experience will echo theirs in more than one sense. His book promises to be a fascinating read. As well as telling his life story, who would bet against it also settling a few scores in his trademark style?

Rupert Murdoch was born 16 years before Lord Sugar, so he can offer a potential guide for the next two decades of Sugar's life. As we have seen, the pair's paths have crossed numerous times and they have collaborated successfully on business deals. As Murdoch entered his sixties, he was forced to weather several storms in his business affairs. His Australia-based firm News Corp was in debt and he had to sell several magazines. Then his Fox Network came under the eye of the US Federal Communications Commission, though the investigation found in his favour. The Fox News Channel then took on the mighty CNN and many of its viewers.

Murdoch continues to chase business success, taking a stake in Hughes Electronics in 2003 and buying the social networking website MySpace two years later. He continues to be an enormously influential figure in the political world too. His publications have often surprised readers by swinging to new political positions, such as the *New York Post*'s backing of Barack Obama and *The Sun*'s swing to the Conservatives in 2009. In short, Murdoch is an example to Lord Sugar that he can have many years of business power and influence ahead of him if that is what he wants.

There are other figures whose stories are worth consulting. Known as the world's greatest investor, Warren Buffett is an example to us all as he lives energetically into his seventies. Despite the billions he owns, he continues to work. Buffett has just one personal assistant, drives himself to and from work and avoids meetings. His office is a simple affair. 'I've never had a computer in there, I've never had a calculator in there, I've never had a stock ticker in there,' he boasts. Of an evening he likes few things more than a simple ham sandwich and a game of online bridge – his username is T-Bone. He knows he will have to appoint a successor one day but is in no hurry to do so and will not be doing so until he is ready to leave. There will be no handover period. 'I mean, what would they do?' he says. 'Come and sit in my office all day, so I could chuck them the paper to read when I'd finished with it?'

So there is no need for Sugar to fear he has to slow down if he does not want to. Fellow Englishman Richard Branson is just three years Sugar's junior and therefore perhaps the closest equivalent. In recent times Branson has become something of an environmentalist, setting up the Virgin Earth Challenge, a prize to encourage green initiatives. He has also championed homeopathic and other alternative health remedies. He continues to pursue world records in numerous challenges, including the crossing of the Atlantic. Although Lord Sugar enjoys physical challenges, including his cycling, one cannot imagine him taking on so many life-threatening adventures as Branson – even if his wife allowed him to indulge himself so dangerously.

One area of business Sugar looks set to remain in is property, as he continues to trade in this market. He has enjoyed dealing in property since 1985 when he formed Amsprop, his real-estate company. His dealings in this sphere, too, have been unconventional, as might be expected. And highly impulsive: colleagues were frequently ordered to close a deal within an hour to buy buildings worth millions of pounds that Sugar had not even visited. 'Everybody has a good laugh at me, because they cannot believe the way I go about doing property deals. I buy and sell properties without even going to look at them,' he said back then. His approach was also governed by a basic rule that he would not bother with any property worth less than £2 milllion.

Although he has purchased numerous grand properties, one of the deals that gave him the most pleasure was for a far more humble address. 'One of the greatest buildings I ever bought was a warehouse on the intersection of the M25 and A12, 15 years ago,' he recalled. 'I paid £800,000 for it. My advisers told me I was stupid and my Jewish advisers called me a schmuck. But for ten years it has been paying me more than £500,000 a year in rent.' As ever, Sugar has savoured the sweet taste of vindication.

Which is why he is set to continue dealing property. In the summer of 2009 he bought a five-star hotel reportedly worth £35 million – for just £2million. The Hotel Byblos on the Costa de Sol, Spain, is a popular haunt for the rich and famous – guests have included Diana Princess of Wales, JK Rowling, Chris Evans and the Rolling Stones. The place had gone bust in recent times, a fact that Sugar leapt on in order to secure it at a knockdown price.

Sugar's son Daniel said: 'I can confirm that Amsprop Espana, a subsidiary of Amshold Limited, has reached an agreement with the courts of Fuengirola regarding three plots of land in Mijas. The legal procedural process is not due to be completed until the start of September. We have no further comment.'

A source told the *News of the World*: 'Lord Sugar is delighted to have acquired this hotel. This really is a belting deal for his empire. He may now be a peer and TV star but he will always remain an entrepreneur at heart.'

A successful one, too – and therein may lie one of his most positive legacies. In contrast to America, success has rarely been celebrated in England. This is a country where spectacular failures like ski-jumper Eddie 'the Eagle' Edwards are treated as heroes but golfing winners like Nick Faldo are regarded with jealousy. When the English football team continually fail at international tournaments, often in the dreaded penalty shoot-out, they are regarded as noble runners-up rather than serial failures. Indeed, key figures in those failures have enjoyed renewed cultural iconic status as a result – see the cases of Paul Gascoigne and Gareth Southgate in particular.

Britain has for so long been comfortable with failure. This is a country that produced the poet Rudyard Kipling, who encouraged readers to treat triumph and disasters as 'impostors' in exactly the same way, a country whose most stirring battle poem is, as George Orwell pointed out, 'about a brigade of cavalry which charged in the wrong direction'. Meanwhile, as the *Daily Telegraph* pointed out in 1987, 'despite ... the rise of a new species of working class entrepreneurs like Alan Sugar, most of Britain's largest fortunes remain in the hands of the landed aristocracy.'

More recently, however, the British have become more comfortable with success. Lord Sugar is a major influence in this change. Britain's increasing ease with success and (deserved) wealth will be one of his finest legacies. It is, in a sense, time to speak of legacies. 'It's a different world and I've got no bloody patience for it,' said Sugar of how times have changed since he started. 'Let the youngsters get on with it, let them talk in their language. I'm not going in the front line any more because I'll end up whacking someone.' In the final analysis, even for mega-ambitious Sugar, there are more important things in life.

Summing up why he has worked so hard all his life, Sugar's explanation was simple – it was for his family. 'Absolutely, of course. That's normal, right? I mean, why did I start out doing all this stuff? It's to make sure my family were secure. Yeah, of course.'

If Sugar can make one more contribution to his country, he will most likely want to inject a new sense of positivity and motivation into a somewhat beaten Britain. The credit crunch has knocked the confidence of many. 'A lot of people believe it is damaging the nation's spirits because of the headlines they are reading in the papers every day. We are in danger of talking ourselves into a recession,' he said. 'There are a lot of companies out there who are just getting on with it instead of jumping on the bandwagon. There is too much doom and gloom about and we need to move on from that.'

We do indeed, and Lord Sugar is our man to make that happen. Often in biographies there is a tendency to conclude that there are two versions of the person who is being written about: the public and the private version. Sometimes, a strikingly different figure emerges during the book. However, Lord Sugar is one of the more consistent characters around. In public and private, on and off camera, he lives his life much the same: with honesty and passion. No wonder nobody has been able to uncover a skeleton in his closet. With him what you see is, largely, what you get.

This might not make for a sensational conclusion to the story, but it makes for an uplifting one. For that is what Sugar is in the final analysis: a man who motivates and whose story brings cheer. When David Thomas concluded his brilliant book *Alan Sugar – The Amstrad Story*, he declared that proving the business doubters wrong 'is one of the main forces driving him forward'.

After more than 40 years in business, Sugar has surely proved his doubters and critics wrong. 'I've been in business since I was a 12-year-old school kid really,' he has said. 'If there was an opportunity and a demand, I'd be there.' He has been there ever since, to the delight of his supporters, family and friends. However, if the sweet taste of vindication over his sourest critics is what motivates Sugar, then his entry into politics provides him with grist galore to his motivational mill. As people line up to criticise him, Sugar will delight in swatting them down and will endeavour always to move onwards and upwards. It is men such as Lord Sugar who make Britain great.